GW00578018

AIRFIX
magazine guide 18

USAAF Camouflage
of
World War 2

Jerry Scutts

Patrick Stephens Ltd
in association with Airfix Products Ltd

First published — 1976

ISBN 0 85059 233 X

More Airfix Magazine Guides for aircraft enthusiasts!

No 1 *Plastic Modelling*
by Gerald Scarborough
No 2 *Aircraft Modelling*
by Bryan Philpott
No 6 *RAF Fighters of World War 2*
by Alan W. Hall
No 10 *Luftwaffe Camouflage of World War 2*
by Bryan Philpott
No 11 *RAF Camouflage of World War 2*
by Michael J. F. Bowyer
No 14 *American Fighters of World War 2*
by Alan W. Hall
No 16 *Modelling Jet Fighters*
by Bryan Philpott

Cover design by Tim McPhee

Text set in 8/9 Helvetica Medium by Blackfriars Press Limited, Leicester.
Printed on Fineblade cartridge 90 gsm and bound by the Garden City Press, Letchworth, Herts.
Published by Patrick Stephens Limited, Bar Hill, Cambridge, CB3 8EL, in association with Airfix Products Limited, London SW18

Contents

Editor's introduction

What were the typical markings of an 8th Air Force Mustang in 1944, or a 9th Air Force Liberator in 1942? Read this book and you can easily find out, together with the markings of every type of major combat aircraft used by the US Army Air Forces at any particular time during World War 2.

For the very first time, aviation enthusiasts and modellers have a quick and easy reference to the basic camouflage schemes and colours, unit symbols, codes and other artwork painted on American Army aircraft of the last war. If you see a photograph of a B-17 in standard Olive Drab and Neutral Grey finish, with a white triangle above the serial number on its fin, then this book will readily inform you that that aircraft belonged to the 97th Bomb Group, 12th Air Force, post-July 1943. It's as accurate and detailed as that. Indeed, if the aircraft could also be seen to be carrying a black number on a white disc, you could also identify the squadron within the Group.

For modellers the book will prove invaluable in authenticating colour schemes before applying them to their plastic construction kits, while the student of aircraft marking schemes could not put his hands on a more concise overall guide to the complex and colourful insignia used by USAAF aircraft.

Following an introductory section which outlines the basic colours and system of applying markings, the book is divided into concise entries on each type of aircraft used, ranging from the Airacobra, Lightning, Mustang and Thunderbolt to the Liberator, Fortress and Mitchell, and including British types in USAAF service such as the Beaufighter, Mosquito and Spitfire. Under each aircraft heading is a list of the Air Forces with which it flew, describing the basic markings of the Force itself, the Groups within it, and the squadrons within the Groups, so that it is a simple matter to look up the appropriate marking scheme for virtually any USAAF aircraft of the war.

The numerous photographs and drawings illustrate typical applications of these schemes at particular times and in different theatres, ranging from Europe and North Africa to China and the Pacific Ocean, making this book an essential reference source for everyone interested in the aircraft of World War 2.

BRUCE QUARRIE

Acknowledgements

In preparing this necessarily brief coverage of the camouflage and markings of the aircraft of the wartime United States Army Air Forces, I have consulted many works of reference by specialists in a number of fields. It is to writers of the calibre of Kenn Rust, Roger Freeman, William Hess, Steve Birdsall, Eric Munday, Bob Pukala and countless others that anyone interested in American aviation owe so much. To them all, may I offer a vote of thanks for the constant inspiration and pleasure generated through their work. I would also like to thank Paul D'Orley for the loan of books and my wife Andrea for constant encouragement and help in typing the manuscript. Should anyone care to correct, update or add to the material in this book, I would be happy to hear from them at 20B Kidbrooke Grove, Blackheath, London SE3 0LF.

General paint finishes and markings

The major section of this book covers the markings of the leading combat aircraft of the United States Army Air Forces, listed under the air forces to which they were assigned.

Apart from the most widely used camouflage colours of Olive Drab upper surfaces and Neutral Grey undersides, Sand, a light stone shade with a pink hue, was used as an upper surface colour in desert areas, while black over all surfaces was specified for night fighters.

Camouflage was instituted before the US entry into the war and, on December 7 1941, most combat aircraft had already been painted. On Army aircraft, the branch of service was identified by the wording 'US ARMY' in black capital letters on the underside of both wings. With the application of camouflage, Type 1 national insignia — introduced by the Air Corps on January 1 1921 — was painted on the fuselage of US aircraft for the first time. Insignia was also removed from the upper surface of the starboard wing and lower surface of the port wing.

Type 1 insignia was used until a directive of May 15 1942 ordered the red centre spot to be removed from the white star to avoid any confusion with the national insignia of Japan.

With Type 2 insignia in use, the next change was on October 1 1942, when the yellow surround was specified to make the star and blue circle more visible. Officially, this surround was to be two inches (5.08 cm) wide, although this did vary. As early as July 1942, such a marking was used in the UK, where a surround to the US marking had been left during the overpainting of RAF roundels on certain types.

By 1943, with future war plans likely to involve the overflying by USAAF aircraft of countries not directly involved in the conflict, the application of the US flag was recommended as an additional recognition aid, following an order of January 19. Many machines used in the early stages of the 'Operation Torch' landings in North Africa were to be seen with the flag marked on their vertical tail surfaces and under the port wing.

A further marking of MTO US aircraft was the RAF fin flash, used as an

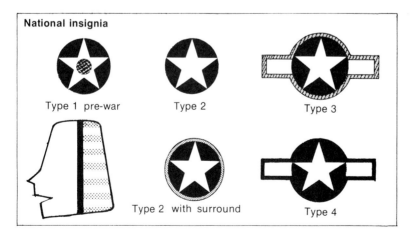

National insignia

Type 1 pre-war   Type 2   Type 3

Type 2 with surround   Type 4

Allied theatre identification marking following an order to that effect in December 1942.

Bars to the star

After detailed tests in the US in mid-1943, the American insignia was again revised by the addition of two horizontal white rectangles on each side of the star and circle, the top lines of which were level with the horizontal arms of the star. The rectangles, or 'bars', were to be continued out for one circle radius on each side and were to be one half radii deep. The reason for this move was to present the US insignia as a *rectangle* from a distance. As the tests showed, the star marking tended to blur into a mere circle at a distance, as did the German cross and Japanese 'meatball'. By adding bars, the American marking was given a more immediately recognisable shape. Orders were issued to make the change on June 28 1943, to be fully implemented by not later than September 1 1943.

Before the deadline for the new marking, however, which brought back red into the national insignia in the form of a surround one eighth of the radius wide, a counter order, dated August 14 1943 changed the border colour to blue. This followed complaints over the use of red from the Pacific theatre, where it was felt that that shade could still cause confusion with the Japanese marking.

As the latter directive began to be complied with in the combat zones, many aircraft could be seen with a darker surround to the faded blue disc where the fresh red surround had been overpainted with blue. The directive of August 14 also stated that where the insignia was painted on a very dark background, no border — or blue circle — would need to be painted. Also, where camouflage was deemed important to an aircraft's mission, the white areas could be dulled with light grey. This practice had, of course, been used for some time before the official directive.

The next major change in overall finish of USAAF aircraft came about early in 1944 when a directive dated February 13 stated that 8th AF fighters and strategic bombers would no longer use overall camouflage. Apart from OD anti-glare sections forward of cockpits and engine panels immediately within the pilot's vision on multi-engined types, the majority of US aircraft would henceforth be in natural metal finish.

However, in certain areas and on particular types, camouflage was retained. In the Pacific especially, some aircraft were in the standard paint scheme until the last day of the war, while others had been phased out of production before NMF was generally adopted in the factories.

Removal of camouflage paint was initially carried out at depots in the combat theatres until NMF machines arrived direct from the US. Even then,

Key to mission symbols on facing page

1 *Bomb mission as lead crew.* 2 *Lead crew (variation).* 3 *Bomb with target name.* 4 *Bombing mission (variation).* 5 *V-weapons site raid.* 6 *Camera — photo mission.* 7 *Broom — fighter sweep.* 8 *Umbrella — top cover.* 9 *Top hat and cane — fighter escort.* 10 *Purple Heart — crew member wounded in action.* 11 *Paradrop.* 12 *Airborne troop drop.* 13 *Japanese meatball — aircraft kill.* 14 *Swastika — German aircraft kill.* 15 *Swastika (variation).* 16 *Rising Sun flag — Japanese aircraft kill.* 17 *Red Cross — Medevac mission.* 18 *Patee Cross — German aircraft kill (variation).* 19 *Iron Cross — German aircraft kill.* 20 *Italian aircraft kill.* 21 *Enemy aircraft destroyed — usually Pacific theatre.* 22 *Ships sunk.* 23 *Duck — decoy mission.* 24 *Bombing mission (variation).* 25 *Camel — mission over the 'Hump' or Himalayas.* 26 *Train destroyed.* 27 *Mountain — hump mission (variation).* 28 *Shell — mission record (variation).* 29 *Swastika with red ring — kill.* 30 *German flag — kill.* 31 *Bridge destroyed.* 32 *Eye — photo mission.* 33 *German aircraft kill.* 34 *Top cover/bombing mission.* 35 *Boxcar — cargo carrier mission.*

field commanders would have certain categories of aircraft repainted, often using local, rather than American, paints. This was particularly true in the ETO and MTO, where upper surface green paint was thought necessary for tactical aircraft. Many 8th, 9th and 12th Air Force fighters and medium bombers were consequently re-sprayed on their upper surfaces, and often retained tactical camouflage until the end of the war.

On April 18 1944 the directive that led to the application of black and white Allied recognition stripes for the invasion of France was first circulated. It stipulated that these markings should make aircraft 'more easily identified as friendly by ground and naval forces and by other friendly aircraft'.

The invasion, or Allied Expeditionary Air Forces, black and white stripes would, the official directive stated, apply to all categories of aircraft except four-engined bombers and seaplanes but not, strangely, for these *were* so painted, to transports, gliders and night fighters.

The markings were to become effective 'as shortly before the day of the assault as it is possible to protect the effectiveness of their use' and remain 'until it is deemed advisable to change'. On single-engined types, the stripes were directed to be applied as white/black/W/B/W, 18 inches (45.72 cm) wide, parallel to the longitudinal axis of the aircraft on upper and lower wing surfaces, the sequence to read from the centre outwards. Stripes were to start 6 inches (15.24 cm) inboard of the national insignia.

On the fuselage, stripes were stipulated to be of similar width and sequence as those around the wings and with the outer edge of the rearmost band 18 inches (45.72 cm) from the leading edge of the tailplane.

On twin-engined aircraft, stripes were to be 24 inches (60.96 cm) wide on both wings and fuselage and located similarly to those of single-engined categories, the larger width also applying to glider tugs and transports.

Stripes were to be in 'no case applied over national markings or special equipment, such as de-icer boots'. The directive stated that the choice of paint be left to the Commanding General of the Air Force in the case of American aircraft.

Black and white stripes were also used in the Pacific for recognition purposes for another invasion — that of the Philippines in October 1944. Single-engined fighters received wing and fuselage bands over both NMF and OD. They varied from 24 inches (60.96 cm) to 36 inches (91.44 cm) wide and were usually applied as two black fuselage bands (occasionally one) and two wing bands, although examples were to be seen with one and three wing bands. On NMF, the white bands were not always used, but the black markings remained in use until the end of the war.

Type recognition markings
On February 20 1943 white identity markings were advised for Republic P-47 Thunderbolts in Britain to avoid confusion with the Fw 190. These were a 24 inch (60.96 cm) engine cowling band, a 12 inch (30.48 cm) horizontal fin/rudder stripe and 18 inch (45.72 cm) bands around the tailplane. Additionally, national insignia was to appear in all four wing positions.

P-51 Mustangs received similar markings to distinguish them from the Bf 109 following an order of December 20 1943: white spinner and 12 inch (30.48 cm) nose band, 15 inch (38.10 cm) wing bands approximately 15 feet (457.20 cm) from the tips, a 12 inch (30.48 cm) horizontal fin/rudder band and a 15 inch (38.10 cm) band around each tailplane.

To avoid confusion with the Kawasaki Ki-61 Tony, 5th AF directed that from September 1943 all single-engined fighters would have white tail surfaces and wing leading edges. The tail marking was brought forward on to the rear fuselage to terminate in a straight or horizontally back or forward sloping line. These markings were used until late 1944, when many aircraft were given pre-war type rudder striping in red and white, usually divided into 13 horizontal stripes. A vertical Insignia Blue stripe preceded the red and white stripes.

Although not strictly in the type recognition category, the striking 8th AF formation leader B-24s were painted up especially to be noticed. At least a dozen Liberator groups used brightly marked aircraft — usually 'war weary' B-24Ds — as an aid to formation assembly over England, some using up to two or three aircraft in this role. Older aircraft were replaced by newer B-24J and H models which often carried similar markings. Paint schemes varied from the jazzy red horizontal 'lightning flashes' on NMF for the 466th BG to the half white/half OD polka-dotted ships of the 458th BG. To enhance their visibility, many of these aircraft were fitted with flashing lights.

Mission markings
The practise of applying symbols to record the number of missions flown by and the combat credits of a particular aircraft or pilot was extremely popular in the wartime USAAF, to the extent that the scoreboard became almost a standard marking in some units.

Mission symbols were generally painted on the forward fuselage, their location usually being dictated by the design of the aircraft. The lower cockpit canopy framing of P-51s was favoured by many pilots to record kills, whereas C-47 Skytrain crews often applied the record of their operations aft of the cockpit or above the cabin windows.

Symbols were usually white or yellow on OD and black on NMF and took many different forms. Stencils were used, although many squadrons relied on the skill of a crewman with a brush. On bombers, if a target was considered particularly 'rough', the name of the city would be painted on the relevant bomb silhouette. Some crews also put the target name on each bomb as a matter of course.

A significant milestone in an aircraft's combat career was often recorded as an extra large or differently coloured bomb symbol to denote 25, 50 or 100 missions. Bomber gunners' victories were often painted near their station, along with their name.

Squadron badges, approved before or during the war or generated at squadron/group level without official sanction, were applied quite extensively in some theatres, especially the Pacific.

What is commonly known as 'nose art' took an infinite variety of forms — very often female — colours and positions on American aircraft and ranged from a simple name to the striking nose-to-tail artwork seen on some Pacific-based B-24s. The name, artwork and mission record were usually grouped together on the noses of bombers, fighters often having a name on the nose and the score close to the cockpit. With *any* paint scheme or marking however, there were a vast number of exceptions to the basic 'rules' — a fact that should always be borne in mind by anyone attempting to determine the 'correct' finish of wartime aircraft.

USAAF aircraft

Bell P-39 Airacobra

5th Air Force Airacobras in standard camouflage were identified by numbers — 1-9 for headquarters aircraft and 10-39, 40-69 and 70-99 for the first, second and third squadrons in a group.

Each squadron of the 8th FG applied an aircraft letter on the nose of P-39s, in white or the unit colour, which also appeared on the spinner, as a thin vertical nose band — usually over the armament access door — or as a band on the tip of the vertical tail surfaces. Both nose and tail markings were used on some aircraft, as were pre-war command stripes — two for a squadron commander, one for a flight commander — usually painted around the centre fuselage, aft of the dorsal intake in white. On the white theatre tail markings, serials were either left in yellow on an OD patch, or repainted in black.

Whereas the 8th FG used letter identification, the 35th FG and 82nd and 110th Squadrons of the 71st TRG used numbers, although early 35th Group P-39s also had ID letters, situated aft of the exhaust stacks. Numbers were either on nose or tail and the tip of the fin/rudder was trimmed in the squadron colour: blue for the 39th FS, red for the 40th and yellow for the 41st. Spinners were usually left in OD.

7th, 11th and 13th Air Forces Early camouflaged P-39s were identified by serials and numbers in blocks approximately the same as those used by the 5th Air Force, and were usually placed on the nose.

Of the 675 Airacobras ordered for the RAF, 179 were transferred to the USAAF as P-400s, most retaining their British-type camouflage of Dark Green/Dark Earth with Sky (Type S) undersides and spinners, the paints used being of US manufacture and not matching British shades exactly. The serials of those aircraft that were marked prior to diversion to the USAAF were positioned under the tailplane in black, and were in the ranges AH750-'739, AP264-'384, BW100-'183 and BX135-'434.

Some British order P-39s reached the 67th FS, 347th FG, on Guadalcanal between August 1942 and June 1943. They had white ID fin numbers, distinctive sharkmouths and white wingtips. Some aircraft also carried the 67th's Walt Disney 'Fighting Gamecock' squadron badge on their cockpit doors.

Only basic camouflage and serials were carried by most Airacobras of the

Bell P-400s on Guadalcanal. The nearest machine still carries the RAF serial BW167, with a white plane-in-squadron number '6' on the fin, white wingtips and Type 1 national insignia.

USAAF camouflage of World War 2

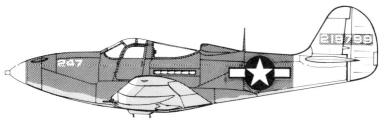

Pacific area recognition markings shown on P-39N 42-18799. White tailplane and wing leading edge. Fuselage demarcation lines were often diagonal and wing leading edges were occasionally in bare metal.

Bell P-39M 42-4724 of the 93rd FS running up its engine at Hergla, Tunisia, with heavy engine exhaust doing nothing for its codes or national insignia! (Howard Levy).

7th and 11th Air Forces, although many had distinctive nose art and names.

12th Air Force The 31st and 350th Groups joined the 12th after original assignment to the 8th Air Force and the 81st and 322nd Groups were assigned directly, along with the 68th Reconnaissance Group.

Both P-39s and P-400s were used in the MTO, squadron identification in the 81st FG being by single letter placed forward of the national insignia, with an aircraft letter aft, the 93rd FS being known to have used 'Q'. Desert theatre aircraft were subject to much local repainting, and this, together with prolonged exposure to the weather, often resulted in unusual mottled effects. Yellow theatre wing markings were applied on P-39s from 1943.

Bristol Beaufighter

12th Air Force Beaufighter Mks IVF (with AI Mk IV radar) and X (AI Mk VIII in a thimble nose radome) were used

by four USAAF night fighter squadrons in 1943, the 414th, 415th, 416th and 417th. Some 40 aircraft, in the BT, KW and V serial ranges, were transfer-

Bristol Beaufighter Mk VI V8694 at Gerbini, Sicily in late 1943. The aircraft has had its tail repainted and bears the last two digits of the serial on the rudder in white. There are no surrounds to the national insignia bars and the aircraft was similar on the reverse side (Howard Levy).

red from RAF stocks in standard camouflage of Medium Sea Grey overall with Dark Green camouflage on the top surfaces.

British markings were overpainted in Dark Green or Olive Drab, the US insignia sometimes being applied on the top surfaces of both wings, approximately in the position of the RAF roundels. Removal of the fin flash often extended to the respraying of the entire tail unit in grey and being

brought forward to a point bisected by the rearmost national insignia bars on both sides of the fuselage.

RAF serials remained in most cases, the last two digits occasionally being repeated at the top of the vertical fin for radio call purposes. Some machines are also believed to have had coloured propeller bosses and at least one, Mk X KW417 of the 415th Squadron, had a red, white and blue rudder trim tab.

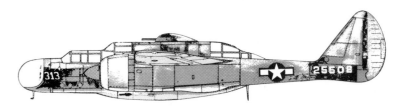

Northrop P-61A 42-5508 of the 419th NFS, 13th AF. Camouflage was very weathered OD and Neutral Grey, with yellow serials. White '313' and radome.

Northrop P-61 Black Widow
5th, 7th, 10th and 13th Air Forces

Both OD and NG and black-finished P-61s served in the CBI and Pacific theatres, the majority having the latter shade. Squadrons of the 5th and 13th Air Forces are believed to have been the only ones to have applied unit markings.

Aircraft of the 5th AF's 418th NFS had a white tail marking: a crescent at the top of the rudder with a small star on the lower fin, linked by two diagonal stripes, the topmost of which ended just short of a small triangle. A number of P-61s of the 547th NFS had alternate engine cooling gills painted white, as well as portions of the spinners.

Aircraft of the 13th AF's 550th NFS were identified by the unit's 'Stalking Cat' emblem under the cockpit and horizontal fin/rudder stripes in the squadron colour, green, edged with white.

Some aircraft of the 419th NFS on Guadalcanal in 1945 used italic style three-digit plane-in-squadron num-

bers on the nose, similar to those employed by the 550th Squadron, which carried them on the fin. Some P-61s of the latter unit also had diagonal rear boom bands in white.

9th and 12th Air Forces Early production matt black finished P-61s were delivered to the 422nd NFS in the ETO starting March 1944. However, due to the fact that matt paint was found to show up the aircraft as a grey silhouette in searchlight beams, standard OD and grey was substituted, at least until the development of a suitable gloss black. By late 1943, tests proved that the momentary reflection from gloss paint was far more acceptable for night fighter use and a shade known as 'Jet' was standardised for P-61s.

Both matt black and OD-finished P-61s were in use in the ETO when AEAF stripes were applied for D-Day. Most machines had the stripes only on their wing and boom undersurfaces, although some had them completely encircling booms and wings. Usually the stripes terminated at a point approximately in line with the centre

Northrop P-61As of the 422nd NFS, 9th Air Force. Nearest the camera is 42-5536 in camouflage finish, with 42-5564 'Jukin Judy' in the lead and 42-5573 aft, both in black gloss paint. The white spot on the rudder of '573 appears to have been a personal marking to match the heart on the nose.

of the national insignia bar on the boom sides.

Even though it hardly showed up on black, the Insignia Blue surround to the national markings was applied to Black Widows. On gloss black aircraft serials were red, but yellow was used on matt and OD-finished machines.

B-17 Flying Fortress

5th, 7th and 10th Air Forces Most B-17s that saw action against the Japanese were camouflaged, some in OD and NG, but others were given coats of any green paint available. Shadow shading is known to have been used, the colours including Olive Drab, Sand, Medium Green, Dark Brown and green — in two or more

Boeing B-17E 'Alabama Exterminator II' dispersed, awaiting the next operation with the 97th BG. An early aircraft in Earth and green camouflage, it has Sky undersides and rear fuselage and wheel hub emblems. Note how the topside green paint is taken right round the cowling rings.

Nose art and mission symbols adorn B-17E 42-30721 of the 533rd BS, 381st BG. The name, 'last three' of the serial and Boeing project number P22 are in yellow, with bomb symbols in white. Dark blue inverted triangles indicate strikes on 'Noball' V-weapon sites in front of the squadron badge, a 'Death's Head' in a knight's helmet and plume, over a diagonal bomb, all on a black disc outlined yellow.

combinations of those shades.

No unit markings were used, aircraft identification being by serial number, the last two or three digits of which were repeated on the nose and occasionally, immediately behind the cockpit windows.

No NMF Fortresses are known to have seen combat in the Pacific, although a number without overall paintwork were used on liaison duties.

8th Air Force RAF-type shadow shading was also a feature of some of the first B-17s sent to Britain in mid-1942, with Dark Earth patterns applied over Olive Drab. Undersides were often in Deep Sky, a shade that appears to have been nearer Azure Blue than the 'duck egg green' associated with British Sky. 'Sky Gray', the US equivalent of Sky Type S, was also used on early B-17E and F models. Some aircraft had portions of their upper surfaces oversprayed with Medium Green in irregular, blotched patterns to break up their outline.

Tail serials were initially the sole means of identification, with the last two digits repeated on the nose in ID Yellow. 'US ARMY' appeared under the wings of the first 8th AF B-17s, along with a thin chordwise coloured band at each wingtip breakpoint. Some machines also had decorated mainwheel hub cover plates.

As deliveries built up, OD and NG was standardised upon, the use of Medium Green blotching gradually being dropped. By late 1942 the B-17s of the 8th had adopted yellow plane-in-squadron letters on the fin, either above or below the serial, and three letter squadron and individual aircraft code letters on the fuselage. Light Grey, albeit in varying shades, became the standard colour for these codes, the positioning of which ranged from being split by the national insignia in the majority of units to being grouped together aft or forward of it. Some groups did not use the letter 'I', while others used it to indicate the second aircraft with the same ID code in a

USAAF camouflage of World War 2

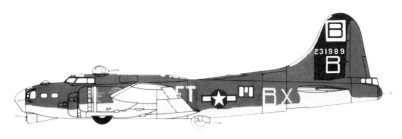

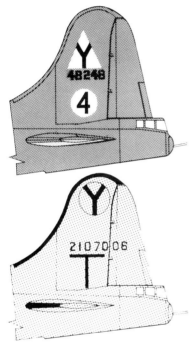

Above *OD and grey camouflaged B-17G 42-31989 of the 336th BS, 95th BG, 8th AF, coded ET-B — previously 'X' as can be seen from the faded letter on aft fuselage. Codes were light grey, serial yellow. Dark area on centre fin was standard on B-17s, being in Medium Green, rather than OD. Fin letter was yellow.* **Left** *Tail markings of camouflaged B-17G 44-8248 of the 414th BS, 97th BG, 15th Air Force. White symbols, black serial, symbol and squadron-in-group number.* **Below left** *Natural metal finished B-17G 42-107006 of the 49th BS, 2nd Bomb Group, 15th Air Force. Black markings.*

facing sections of the engine cowlings and on some machines, the top of the 'long' tail gun position in front of the gunner's window, being left as OD anti-glare panels. With the removal of camouflage, colour markings came into increasing use, usually supplementing existing wing/group identification. Mostly, these were confined to the tail area of the B-17s, but chin turrets and the forward nose area, wings and propeller bosses were included in many cases — indeed, the painting of the latter in squadron colours was the start of one of the most striking combat markings systems of the war, some of which are illustrated throughout this book.

12th and 15th Air Forces The four Fortress groups of the 12th AF in the MTO were in OD and NG finish initially, although some in the ex-8th AF units had two-tone camouflage in Sand and Olive Drab or Medium Green. In the spring of 1943, each group applied a small hollow geometric symbol to the fin of each aircraft

squadron.

To enhance air-to-air identification, geometric fin symbols were introduced in July 1943 — a triangle for the groups in the 1st Combat Bomb Wing, and a square for the 3rd CBW. Within each symbol was a letter for each group in the wing, the whole device being displayed on the fin and the upper starboard wing and, occasionally, the lower port. The symbols were white, often dulled to Light Grey, with Insignia Blue, later black, letters.

On NMF B-17s, white markings were generally changed to black, with the area forward of the cockpit, the inner

Formation of B-17Gs of the 390th BG, showing aircraft of the 568th (code BI), 570th (CC) and 571st (FC) Squadrons with respective red, yellow and green nose bands and yellow group wing bands. Aircraft CC-F at top right has the square C wing marking of the 96th BG.

Names and artwork on the fin fillet were a feature of B-17s of the 463rd BG, 15th AF. 'Joker', 42-31694 has had a late Cheyenne tail position fitted, which had not been painted at the time of this photograph.

above the serial, the shape of which identified the group — a circle for the 2nd BG, a triangle for the 97th, a diamond for the 99th and a square for the 301st. When two new groups were added to the by-then 15th AF B-17 force in the spring of 1944, all six adopted the letter Y as identification.

The four older groups placed the letter on their existing symbols and the 463rd, one of the new arrivals, used a 'pie slice' 60 degree segment of a circle. The other newcomer, the 483rd, had no symbol, but painted a small star at the bottom of the vertical stroke of the Y.

USAAF camouflage of World War 2

Squadron identification took various forms; the 2nd used symbols for three of its four squadrons as well as single wing and rudder bands. A T shape identified the 49th BS, a wide V the 96th and a 'key' device the 429th. The 97th BG used black numbers — the last digit of the squadron number — on a white disc — 0,1,2 and 4 for the 340th, 341st, 342nd and 414th Squadrons, respectively. Roman figures identified the 99th BG's squadrons —

I, II, III and IV for the 346th, 347th, 348th and 416th respectively and the 301st BG used letters — A, B, C and D for the 32nd, 352nd, 353rd and 419th Squadrons.

With NMF, some groups continued to paint the symbol on the upper surfaces of each horizontal tailplane, and rudders were given various horizontal and diagonal designs to further identify squadrons. Coloured rudders were also used at the end of the war.

Douglas A-20 Havoc

5th Air Force Flying combat from August 1942, the 3rd Bomb Group's camouflaged A-20s had basic plane-in-squadron nose numbers and machines of the 90th BS often had sharkmouth markings. Coloured squadron markings appeared as a band on the upper segment of the vertical tail surfaces — yellow for the 8th BS, red for the 13th, green for the 89th and white for the 90th. Where the colour contrast was bad, a thin white band underlined it. Occasionally, the last three digits of the serial were applied to the extreme nose tip. Squadron insignia was applied to A-20Gs of the 13th and 90th Squadrons — a skeletal device for the former and a pair of dice for the latter. The 13th's white 'Grim Reaper' was sometimes placed on the rear fuselage of group aircraft in general, usually with a black background to contrast the white skeleton.

A-20Gs of the 312th BG also carried white ID letters on their rudders, with a white horizontal stripe across both fin and rudder. White playing card symbols on the rear fuselage identified the squadrons — a club for the 386th, a diamond for the 387th, a heart for the 388th and a spade for the 389th. In addition a white skull and (sometimes) crossed bones was painted on the nose tip, with the upper pair of machine-guns protruding through the eyes of the skull.

Third of the 5th AF's Havoc units was the 417th BG, which also had white fin ID letters and coloured diagonal sections of the forward upper fin and rudder to distinguish squadrons — red for the 672nd, yellow for the 673rd, white for the 674th and blue for the 675th, all except the 674th adding a contrasting white border.

Two 5th AF night fighter squadrons, the 418th and 421st, used the P-70

Douglas A-20Bs of the 97th BS, 47th BG, 12th AF. Both have the Sand blotching over Olive Drab used by the group for a short time and the nearest aircraft, 41-3014, still bears the squadron badge, a comic white rabbit on a medium blue disc riding a bomb. The aircraft is also named 'Wahoo'. In the background is 41-3134.

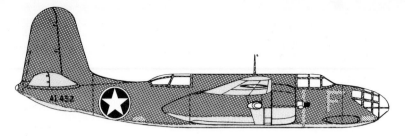

Douglas Boston III AL452 of the 15th BS (Light), 8th Air Force, attached to No 226 Squadron RAF. Aircraft is believed to have had British camouflage overpainted in OD, although RAF red code letter remains. US insignia in standard positions, with yellow surround to fuselage cocarde.

version of the Havoc for a limited period. It is believed that most carried standard camouflage with black undersides, identification being only by serial.

7th and 13th Air Forces Two units, the 7th AF's 6th NFS and the 13th AF's 419th NFS, also flew the P-70 Nighthawk, probably marked similarly to those mentioned above. The handful of Havocs used in the early days of the war are not believed to have carried any unit markings before replacement by other types.

9th Air Force Camouflaged A-20G and J models of the 409th, 410th and 416th Groups joined the 9th AF early in 1944. Yellow serials identified individual aircraft and letter/number

codes were allocated to each group, which also applied rudder stripes as follows — yellow for the 408th, black and white squares for the 410th and white for the 416th.

The long engine nacelles and short depth rear fuselage of the Havoc meant that the individual code had to be smaller than normal and was often obscured by the shadow of the tailplane. In an attempt to offset this problem, the 410th BG began to use cowling colours — red for the 644th BS, white for the 645th, blue for the 646th and yellow for the 647th. Propeller bosses were also painted in some cases.

AEAF stripes were applied to Havocs for D-Day, the actual width and

A-20G 5H-B of the 668th BS, 416th BG, with white rudder stripe. The aircraft still shows the stencil breaks in the code letters and NMF strips at the fin joint, left when the aircraft was assembled and not always overpainted on 9th AF Havocs.

USAAF camouflage of World War 2

A-20B 41-3139 of the 47th BG. Green had by this time been sprayed over the Sand blotching and the 86th BS squadron badge.

positioning varying; when upper surface stripes were deemed no longer necessary, a coat of OD or Dark Green dulled them down sufficiently but both black and white still showed through on many machines.

Some A-20s used on night operations had portions of their undersides finished in Jet Black, others being completely repainted. As well as selected machines from the three bomb groups, Havocs equipped the 155th PRS.

Many Bostons intended for the RAF were impressed into the USAAF early in the war, Mk IIIs being acquired by the 15th BS of the 8th AF as early as August 1942. Where aircraft were repainted in US type camouflage, the use of British paints made for slightly different shades to those of OD and NG. RAF serials were retained and red plane-in-squadron letters were carried on the nose, as per British practice.

12th Air Force The 47th BG was the first complete USAAF A-20 unit overseas, joining the 12th AF late in 1942. Some Olive Drab-finished Havocs of the group were blotched with Sand on their upper surfaces, but this type of camouflage did not endure for long. Unit badges were carried on both sides of the nose by most aircraft of the group when it arrived in the MTO, and these were usually overpainted.

Following use of small plane-in-squadron nose numbers, the 47th introduced white battle numbers on fins and rudders, being crudely hand-painted at first. Each squadron had 25 numbers allocated — 1-24 for the 84th BS, 25-49 for the 85th, 50-74 for the 86th and 75-99 for the 97th. Single numbers were painted on the rudders of the 84th BS machines, and serials were retained in most cases.

Douglas A-26 Invader

5th Air Force The 3rd Bomb Group re-equipped with camouflaged A-26s in 1945 and continued to use markings similar to those of its Havocs, with single white plane-in-group letters on the fin.

7th Air Force When the 12th AF's 319th Bomb Group moved to the Pacific in 1945, its NMF A-26s used the markings of its B-26s and B-25s in the MTO — white battle numbers on black fins and rudders. Two-digit numbers were split across the fin and rudder, although some aircraft with single numbers had only the rudder painted to contrast the white digit. A further presentation was three small black numbers above the serial on the fin on NMF surfaces. On black fins, serials were usually repainted in yellow or white.

9th Air Force NMF A-26s were used by five 9th AF groups; where they replaced B-26s and A-20s, existing rudder tail markings and code letters were perpetuated. The exception was the 410th BG, which had had white

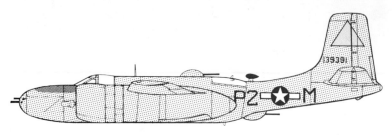

Douglas A-26B Invader 41-39381 of the 572nd BS, 391st BG, 9th Air Force. Overall NMF with OD anti-glare panel, black codes and serial. Black-outlined yellow triangle.

Seen in the US immediately after the war is A-26B 8U-K of the 646th BS, 410th BG, with buzz number BA-178 on the engine cowling (Via R. L. Ward).

rudder stripes on camouflaged A-20s, but which was black on Invaders. Most machines had nose and inward-facing engine cowling panels in anti-glare OD or black and in some cases, extensive exhaust staining led to the entire nacelles being painted.

Invasion stripes were carried on the lower surfaces of some 9th A-26s, particularly those of the 396th BG, which also included examples with squadron colours over their entire engine nacelles, the 553rd BS using yellow.

A few Invaders of the 410th BG used as experimental target marker aircraft in 1945 were black overall, though no codes are believed to have been used.

Some Invaders of the 69th TRG assigned to the 9th AF in 1945 were identified by black two-digit numbers on an orange-yellow fin and rudder band. Wingtips of some aircraft — and

Although Invaders carrying markings similar to these two machines have often been quoted as part of the 9th AF, they were in fact from the 56th Combat Crew Training Wing of the 1st Air Force in the US. Nearest the camera is A-26B 41-39405, W1-F, with Y1-F behind (Via D. Morris).

USAAF camouflage of World War 2

possibly rudders — were in the same colour at the end of the war.

12th Air Force The Havoc-equipped 47th BG received Invaders in 1945, including some black-finished radar-carrying night intruders. NMF machines employed a similar plane-in-squadron identification system to that used on A-20s. However, whereas Havocs had had two-digit numbers split across the fin and rudder, Invader numbers were on the fin above the serial, which was black on NMF and red on black finish.

Consolidated B-24 Liberator

5th Air Force Pacific theatre Liberators initially carried little in the way of ID markings on camouflage finish apart from tail serials. The first to apply unit markings as such was the 90th Bomb Group, the 'Jolly Rogers'. A white skull and crossed bombs was applied to each outer fin, the full serial or its last three digits being repositioned above the skull. When squadron colours came into use in mid-1944, they were presented as a background to the emblem — red for the 319th, blue for the 320th, green for the 321st and black for the 400th. Some machines also applied rudder striping and the 320th Squadron made extensive use of a sharkmouth on both OD and NMF.

The 22nd Bomb Group, the 'Red Raiders', flew both OD and NMF B-24s, identification of squadrons being by coloured horizontal tail bands — yellow for 33rd, blue for the 2nd, white for the 19th and green for the 408th. Single letters or the last three or four digits of the serial gave plane-in-squadron identity but, by late 1944, letters are believed to have been replaced by numbers in all four squadrons. Some machines also carried the large red Viking head 'Raiders' badge under the cockpit.

Standard drab and overall black paintwork was applied to Liberators of the 43rd BG, the latter shade being on aircraft of the 63rd BS, the 'Sea Hawks' which carried an appropriate fin badge below the serial. Standard group markings consisted of a white diagonal fin/rudder stripe on OD, black on NMF. Late in the war, the 65th BS painted a red or black disc on the fin upon which were two dice, showing the numbers '4' and '3' uppermost; the 403rd sported a white (OD) or black (NMF) upper section of the fin and most group aircraft had both the serial and the 'last three' on

B-24Ds of the 8th AF's 2nd Air Division showing well the early markings prior to application of symbols, including Medium Green blotching of the tail surfaces.

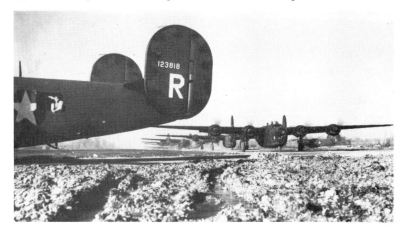

the fin. Rudder striping was also used and some aircraft had the group nickname, 'Ken's Men' on the forward fuselage.

The 380th BG quartered its Liberators' fins and rudders in white to identify squadrons — top forward, 528th BS, bottom forward, 529th BS, top rear, 530th and bottom rear, 531st. Known as the 'Flying Circus' in 1944, the 380th used animal fin designs — elephant and clown for the 528th and 529th, a bomb-carrying monkey for the 530th and a seal balancing a bomb for the 531st. These gave way to a lion's head device on most group aircraft in 1945, squadrons being identified by horizontal rudder stripes —

B-24J 42-50646 GO-L of the 328th BS, 93rd BG with the group code B on the starboard wing. Yellow and black fins/rudders with ID letter in yellow (T. Bennett).

Interesting photograph of Consolidated's Fort Worth production line showing B-24Ds and C-87s in final assembly. The first ten machines have OD and white 'Sea Search' camouflage used by USAAF anti-shipping patrol squadrons. Heading the line are 42-40823 and '835. (USAF).

USAAF camouflage of World War 2

Above *Consolidated B-24J 42-110037 of the 703rd BS, 445th BG, 8th Air Force. OD and grey camouflage, with light grey squadron codes. ID letter and plus sign indicating squadron in group in yellow on fin and fuselage. Yellow serial, black-on-white circle group letter.* **Right** *Tail of 90th Bomb Group, 5th Air Force, B-24D 42-40280. White group symbol and yellow serial. Many of the group's B-24s had their Consolidated tail turrets moved to the nose, giving the impression of later models — this was almost certainly one of those.* **Far right** *Tail of B-24L 44-41419 of the 307th BG, 13th Air Force. 'Long Rangers' symbol white on black, black serial. Tail tip is believed to have been green. NMF overall.*

yellow for the 530th, and probably red, green and blue for the others. In most cases, the last four of the serial appeared on the fin in black.

Also assigned to the 5th AF was the 20th Combat Mapping Squadron, which carried a black winged camera on the fins of NMF B-24s at war's end, often with rudder stripes. The 8th PRS used a black diving hawk device on all-yellow fins, usually below the last four of the serial.

7th Air Force Yellow triangle, square, three horizontal and three vertical bars respectively identified the 26th, 42nd, 98th and 431st Squadrons of the 11th BG's OD-finished aircraft, with the last three digits of the serial repeated on the nose. The full serial remained on the fin, the unit markings (apart from that of the 431st) being painted below it. Black markings were used on NMF.

The 30th BG's 27th, 38th, 392nd and 819th Squadrons are believed to have respectively used a square, disc, vertical bar and horizontal bar in white or black according to finish, serials being retained.

Known as 'Kelly's Cobras', the 494th BG's markings were a black chevron,

diagonal stripe, two vertical bars and solid second and fourth quarters of fin/rudder for the 864th, 865th, 866th and 867th Squadrons respectively. Both full serials and the last three digits were carried on fins.

8th Air Force Early B-24Ds were in OD and NG with upper surfaces blotched in Medium Green in many cases and from late 1942, yellow call letters were applied to the fin, above or below the serial; where a letter duplicated that of another aircraft a bar was added below for a second machine and above for a third.

Group markings were introduced in mid-1943 for 2nd Air Division Liberators when white discs were applied to the top of the fins, upon which was an Insignia Blue or black group letter — A for the 44th, B for the 93rd, C for the 389th and D for the 392nd. Where the call letter was previously above the serial, it was repainted below. Those B-24 groups in the 3rd AD had white square symbols.

Each squadron was assigned a two-letter or letter/number code, which was applied to the rear fuselage in Light Grey, these markings remaining until April 1944, when the 2nd AD received coloured tail markings for its five wings — black for the 2nd, white for the 14th, yellow for the 20th, green for the 95th and red for the 96th. The group within the wing was identified by a single vertical, horizontal or diagonal band, upon which was the aircraft letter and squadron sign, (where allocated) in most cases in the wing colour. Squadron signs were small '+' markings, or '−' signs, under, above, in front of, or behind the ID letter.

Overpainted fin serials were repositioned high on the inside fin surfaces and the white or black disc and group letter remained on the upper starboard wing.

9th Air Force Camouflaged B-24Ds of the Halverson Detachment were the first USAAF Liberators in the MTO, being identified only by serial number and the wording 'US ARMY' under the wings. In July 1942, these aircraft joined B-17s in the 1st Provisional Group and had plane-in-squadron numbers from 10 upwards painted at the top of the fins and extreme forward fuselage.

The first complete B-24 group in the theatre was the 89th, with Sand and NG-finished aircraft, identified by fin and nose letters, which were repeated on the outer engine nacelles. Most machines also had RAF fin flashes as theatre markings, usually below the serial with the call letter adjacent to it.

Some desert Liberators also had two upper wing insignia and unit badges on each side of the nose.

15th Air Force When new B-24 groups joined the ex-9th AF machines in the 15th AF, they were divided into four wings, the 47th, 49th, 55th and 304th, each being identified by geometric fin symbols — respectively a triangle, circle, square and diamond. To identify groups, numbers from 1-4 were applied in black on white discs. The wing symbol appeared at the top of the fin, that for the group at the extreme lower.

Colour markings were introduced in 1944 by the 98th and 376th Groups in the form of vertical rudder and horizontal elevator stripes, and black/-

NMF B-24H of the 304th Bomb Wing, 15th AF, probably of the 455th BG. Serial number 41-28914 with call number 506 on nose. The black fin diamond identified the wing.

white/black rudder and elevator bars respectively. The 449th applied an A device to rudders and the 450th, solid white rudders, all markings mentioned being additional to wing and group symbols.

New colour markings introduced in April 1944 generally perpetuated the old symbols, each wing being given a colour — black and yellow for the 47th, red for the 49th, yellow and black for the 55th and none for the 304th, although the latter used group colours.

The 47th BW continued to use a diagonal division of the lower fin for its groups' markings — yellow/black bars for the 98th, solid black for the 376th, half black/half yellow for the 449th and yellow/black vertical bars for the 450th. Later, all wings repeated fin/rudder markings on the upper surfaces of the tailplane.

The 49th BW's Liberators had the top half of the fin/rudder in solid red, with a red disc, bar and 'bow tie' device for the 451st, 461st and 484th Groups respectively.

The 55th BW's groups divided the vertical tail half yellow (upper) and half black (lower), with a solid black square on the yellow section and yellow group markings in the lower section — a circle for the 460th, vertical bar for the 464th, horizontal bar for the 465th and a cross for the 485th.

USAAF camouflage of World War 2

A 375th BS B-24J, 44-40584 named 'King's X' over the rugged terrain of China. Parent group was the 14th AF's 308th and the rudder stripes are believed to have been black and yellow. The machine has black undersides to its natural metal finish.

As the 55th continued using its original square wing marking, so the 304th perpetuated its diamond in black above the coloured lower section of fin and rudder which identified the groups — white for the 454th, yellow for the 455th, red for the 456th and black/yellow checks for the 459th.

Squadron aircraft within each group were identified in different ways — 47th BW, plane-in-group numbers and letters; 49th BW, numbers 1-19, 20-39, 40-59 and 60-79 for each group squadron; 55th BW, plane-in-group letters; 304th BW, numbers for the 454th and 455th Groups, letters for the 456th and the last digit of the squadron number followed by a letter in the 459th Group — 6, 7, 8, and 9 for the 756th, 757th, 758th and 759th Squadrons respectively.

10th Air Force Both OD and NMF Liberators were used by the 10th AF's sole B-24 unit, the 7th BG. Little is known of early markings, but camouflaged and NMF B-24Js used yellow and black checks respectively on the upper fin surfaces. Large radio call numbers were carried below the marking.

11th Air Force Apart from grey or white plane-in-squadron nose numbers, 11th AF B-24s carried few ID markings on camouflaged finish, some machines of the 404th BS being in Sand as they were originally allocated to the 9th AF. The 21st BS — no 11th AF B-24 units were assigned in group strength — added its unofficial bomb-throwing bumblebee insignia to the noses of some B-24Ds.

13th Air Force The 5th BG, the 'Bomber Barons', identified its aircraft by a white shield shape on dark blue vertical tail surfaces, with a diagonal blue band across it. On NMF, the shield was blue. This marking gave way to hollow geometric symbols — a square for the 23rd BS, and a triangle, circle and diamond for the 31st, 72nd and 394th, although probably not in that order. The 23rd BS also used black plane-in-squadron numbers from 01-25 (approx) and other squadrons are believed to have used succeeding number blocks.

The 307th BG, the 'Long Rangers' flew OD B-24Ds initially, some with the wording 'The Long Rangers' on the fin, along with the last three of the serial repeated on the nose.

On NMF aircraft, the group adopted squadron colours on the fin/rudder tip, with a monogrammed 'LR' on a black disc on the lower fin. Squadron colours were also used to back the group marking in some cases. The last three of the serial appeared on the fuselage nose, sometimes on a contrasting coloured rectangle.

14th Air Force Only B-24 group in China, the 308th flew camouflaged aircraft initially and two squadrons, including the 375th, used three alternate black and white vertical rudder stripes and black and yellow stripes. Extensive use was made of sharkmouth markings in the group, on both OD and NMF aircraft. Two squadrons used diagonal rudder stripes, probably in red and yellow and black and white. Fin serials were generally retained in the 308th and some machines had the 'last three' repeated as plane-in-squadron call numbers. Black undersides were applied to certain machines, usually those with NMF, the demarcation line often being nearly halfway up the fuselage sides, bisecting the national insignia.

P-38 Lightning

5th Air Force Standard OD and NG P-38Fs were received by the 8th FG's 80th FS in February 1943. They were given yellow identification letters on the nose and outer tail surfaces and towards the end of the year, the squadron colour, green, was applied to spinners and the fin and rudder tips, the tailband being edged in white.

By 1944, all 8th FG squadrons had P-38s in NMF, which were identified by letters, then numbers from around 1-20, then letters again, which were used until the war's end. Squadron colours comprised the ID letters, extreme upper and lower fin/rudder tips, forward spinner cones and wing bands in yellow for the 35th FS, these markings usually being edged in black. Letters were often given a black shadow.

Similar markings were used by the 36th FS using black, letters having a thin white outline with a black edging to it. Red was the 80th's colour trim on P-38 H/J/L models, the colour sections being outlined white. ID letters were usually black and command aircraft had extra sections in the squadron colour, often with personal colour markings.

The only squadron of the 35th FG to use P-38s was the 39th which used OD and NG aircraft from late 1942. The numbers 10-39 were painted on the outer fins and fuselage nose pod in white or yellow and sharkmouths were applied to both engine nacelles.

January 1943 saw the 9th FS of the 49th FG using OD and NG P-38Fs, with ID numbers in white or yellow on the fins and fuselage. The group's 7th and 8th Squadrons converted in 1944 and

P-38F of the 48th FS, 14th FG, 8th AF with red squadron commander's stripes on the rear booms. They do not encircle the booms completely, but terminate on a line with the tailplanes. Named 'Wally', this aircraft was probably the machine of the same name flown by Captain W. C. Wallis in North Africa, coded ES. The name appeared on both sides of the nose.

NMF P-38s received colour trim in light blue and black respectively, the 9th using red. Spinner bands, tail tips and fuselage noses were decorated in these colours, no particular system being used. Command pilots' aircraft had larger areas of colour.

The numbers 1-39, 40-69 and 70-99 are believed to have identified the 7th, 8th and 9th Squadrons respectively and these were applied to the nose and boom intake housings. Serial numbers were generally retained.

The 475th FG identified its squadrons by the numbers 110-139, 140-169 and 170-199 for the 431st, 432nd and 433rd respectively, positioning them on the fuselage and fin/rudder surfaces in white on OD finish. Late 1943 colour markings were — red upper fin/rudder tips for the 431st, yellow for the 432nd and white (although light

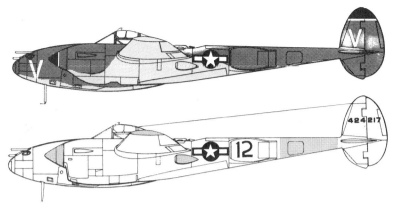

Top *P-38F of the 80th Fighter Squadron, 8th FG, 5th Air Force. Overall OD and grey camouflage with plane-in-squadron letter in yellow. Dark green fin/rudder tip and spinner cone, edged white.* **Above** *P-38L 44-24217 of the 27th FS, 1st FG, 15th Air Force. Red spinners, wingtips, boom bands and fuselage air intake. Black serial, NMF overall.*

blue was used for a time) for the 433rd. Badly contrasting colours were often edged white on OD finish and were also applied to spinners in various patterns. Early in 1944, numbers were painted on each engine nacelle of some machines.

On NMF Lightnings, the 433rd Squadron changed to light blue and colours were used for ID numbers rather than airframe trim, this being in black. Numbers were also outlined black and tail numbers were reduced in size and restricted to the fin when rudder striping was used. From the spring of 1944, the 431st and 432nd Squadrons applied their respective 'Satan's Head' and 'Green clover' badges to the extreme fuselage nose, later moving them to the boom intakes. Diagonal and vertical command stripes encircled the booms of some aircraft, headquarters aircraft being numbered 100-109 and having red/yellow/blue spinners and occasionally, tail tips and rudder striping.

The 6th PR Group's 8th, 25th, 26th and 36th Squadrons flew OD and NG P-38s, F-4s and F-5s, initially identified by the last three digits of the serial on the fuselage nose in yellow or white. The 8th PRS used white two-digit tail numbers and by the end of the war, NMF F-5s had blue/white/red spinners, and upper and lower tail tips, black three-digit engine nacelle numbers, a black 'eightball' with the squadron badge, a black hawk, on a yellow fin disc. Rudder trim tabs were striped in red and white.

7th Air Force It is believed that squadrons of the 18th FG were identified by three-digit fin/rudder numerals and coloured spinners and boom bands in 1945, although exact details are obscure. The 28th PRS flew NMF F-5s at the end of the war, with ID letters on boom intakes, followed by a number, as well as the squadron badge, a cartoon wolf on a light blue disc, on the nacelles.

The 28th then adopted all-black vertical tails with an ID letter on a white or NMF diamond on the fin above the serial, which was also white.

8th Air Force The first P-38s in the ETO in mid-1942 had standard camouflage and serials, with grey constructor's numbers on the extreme fuselage nose in many cases. Both the 1st and 14th FGs numbered aircraft with rear boom command striping, two for a squadron commander, one for a flight commander and painted vertically for A Flight, diagonally forward for B Flight and diagonally backwards for C Flight. In the 1st FG, these bands were red for the 27th FS, white for the 71st and yellow for the 94th.

Code letters, grouped on the boom intakes, were initially pale grey, later white, on 1st FG P-38s; the 14th used Medium Grey letters, often outlined white or yellow. The individual aircraft letter, preceded by a hyphen, was painted aft of the boom intake.

Following the departure of the four original 8th AF groups to the MTO, it was to be August 1943 before the 20th and 55th FGs were to arrive. Aircraft were camouflaged and applied code letters with those for the squadron to the rear of the boom intakes and the ID letter on the intake housing. These codes did not read well and geometric square, circle and triangle symbols to identify squadrons were painted on each outer fin/rudder surface. The aircraft letter was repeated on the inside surface of the vertical tails, white on OD and black on NMF.

The 20th, 364th and 479th Groups applied colour trim to P-38s — yellow and white spinners and forward nacelle bands and red, yellow and blue rudders respectively.

'Droopsnoot' decoy markings were widely used in 1944 — fighter P-38s being given a white fuselage nose band, the area forward of which being highly polished natural metal to give the impression of a perspex-nosed pathfinder aircraft.

AEAF stripes invariably obscured codes on 8th AF P-38s and although tail symbols were 'lifted' around serials in some cases, most machines had them overpainted and identification became virtually impossible.

The first F-4s in the UK were used by the 5th PS in mid-1942 and they initially had standard camouflage. Undersides were soon sprayed with Sky Grey and yellow insignia surrounds were applied prior to the squadron's departure for North Africa. A few F-5s used by the 13th PS in 1943 had OD and NG camouflage, but were soon repainted completely or partially in RAF PRU Blue.

Serials were generally not repainted, the last three being painted on the nose or engine nacelle as radio call numbers, usually in yellow or white. Coloured spinners were used by other PR squadrons assigned to the 8th, but no particular system is known. **9th Air Force** Lightnings of the 9th used a similar marking and code system to that of the 8th, with the exception that AEAF stripes did not cover code letters. Colour markings were also applied in a more random fashion, in various places on the airframe.

Photographic units displayed codes, but rarely individual aircraft letters. PRU Blue was widely used and squadron codes were painted on the boom intakes, with the last three serial digits on the nacelles, in white, black or yel-

P-38J 42-67232 of the 384th FS, 364th FG, 8th AF showing the white recognition square with yellow serial re-applied over it. The 'bar' indicates the second 'W' of the squadron and the last three digits of the serial are repeated on the nose (Via J. Preston).

USAAF camouflage of World War 2

A 12th AF F-4A, 42-364, showing typical weathering of camouflage and insignia. Photographed on Malta, the aircraft has a yellow '64' as plane-in-squadron identity on the nose.

low on PRU Blue and black on NMF.

10th and 14th Air Forces Squadrons of three groups, the 33rd, 51st and 80th, flew P-38s in the CBI theatre, the latter displaying coloured spinners and cowlings on camouflaged F and J models, upon which were painted stylised snakes heads after the 459th FS badge. Dotted white 'snake' outlines were extended down the fuselage of some machines of the 80th Group and plane-in-squadron identification was by three digit fin/rudder numbers. Single horizontal bands — probably in squadron colours — ran below the tailplane stub.

A wide variety of camouflage schemes was seen on photographic F-4s and F-5s in China and India, aircraft identity including cowling and fin numbers in various styles and colours. Letters were also used by one or more units, displayed on the outside fin/rudder surfaces, and boom bands and coloured wingtips were used.

11th Air Force P-38Fs of the 343rd FG were camouflaged with only tail identification, although some aircraft had command strips on the rear booms as well as yellow fuselage nose tips. White ID numbers were introduced in 1943, being applied to the nose. Serials remained and machines of the 54th FS sported the squadron

badge, an orange-yellow fighting lizard, on a blue circular background, to the boom intakes.

12th and 15th Air Forces Those 8th AF P-38 groups reassigned to the 12th carried the codes allocated in the UK for a time, but when the 14th FG received a third squadron, the 37th, the 48th and 49th Squadrons dropped their respective ES and QU codes and used yellow numbers — 1-30 for the 48th, 31-60 for the 49th and 61-90 for the 37th.

The 1st FG continued to use codes — HV (27th FS), LM- (71st FS) and UN (94th FS). Red, white and yellow wingtips were used by the respective squadrons from early 1943.

The 82nd FG's squadrons used a single letter to identify each — A for the 95th, B for the 96th and C for the 97th — followed by an aircraft letter, both being displayed on the boom intakes.

In November 1943, all 12th AF P-38 groups became part of the 15th AF and the 1st FG soon dropped codes and used coloured boom bands — red for the 27th FS, white for the 71st and yellow for the 94th. On NMF, the 71st used a black band. Battle numbers were painted on the boom intakes and were — 1-30 for the 27th, 31-59 for the 71st and 60-90 for the 94th.

Upper fin/rudder bands were used by the 14th FG — white for the 37th FS, red for the 48th and yellow for the 49th, battle numbers being applied to both boom intakes and the nose, often

A P-38J, believed to have been from the 51st FG, at Comilla, India in August 1944. The name 'Melba Lou' appears on the nose and the rudder stripes are probably personal, rather than standard markings. The number '1' may have identified the aircraft in the squadron (Howard Levy).

outlined in white on NMF. Spinners are believed to have been in squadron colours.

At the end of the war, the 82nd FG's squadrons displayed letters in white on a black panel on the boom intakes and the entire fins and rudders were in squadron colours — believed to have been red, white and black for the 95th, 96th and 97th Squadrons respectively. The ID letter or number was repeated on the fin/rudder; when letter combinations (ie AA, BA, CA, etc) were exhausted, numbers were used — A1, B1, C1 and so on.

Photographic Lightnings in the MTO sported various overall finishes and aircraft identity took a number of forms, including spinner colours, and serial digits prominently displayed. F-5s of the 3rd PG had their NMF top surfaces resprayed with OD, three digit white tail numbers serving as individual identification, along with spinner colours.

13th Air Force At least two fighter groups and one reconnaissance group were attached to the 13th, early aircraft invariably being camouflaged in standard shades. Machines of the 67th FS on Guadalcanal in 1943 had white or yellow fin and fuselage nose numbers, as well as sharkmouth designs on each engine nacelle. The 339th FS, also on the 'Canal' at that time, had P-38Fs with white three-digit plane-in-squadron numbers in the 100 range on the lower section of the nose armament access panels. On NMF, numbers were black and spinner colours were applied. Sharkmouths remained until war's end on 339th FS aircraft.

Numbers in the 200-400 range identified Lightnings of the 18th FG and were displayed on the tail of NMF aircraft, along with boom bands in squadron colours. These large size tail numbers were reduced and displayed — in squadron colours — on the fin only at the end of the war and black outlines were applied in some cases. These numbers were also painted on the fuselage nose and the 18th also numbered P-38s with checkerboard boom intakes.

An unidentified P-38 unit that may have been part of the 13th AF carried a skull and flint axe-head badge on engine nacelles and small black boom intake and nose numbers, all known markings being on NMF.

Martin B-26 Marauder

5th Air Force The first USAAF unit to operate the Marauder, and the only one to do so in the Pacific was the 22nd Bomb Group. Early B-26s were camouflaged, with serials aft of the national insignia on the fuselage sides. Few other identification markings were applied, although fin/rudder tips are believed to have been painted in squadron colours shortly before the group large re-equipped with other types, that of the 33rd BS being white.

By early 1943, only the 19th Squadron still flew the Marauder and its NMF aircraft became known as the 'Silver Fleet'. A small black 'winged wheel' with those words upon it was applied to the fins above the black serial.

12th Air Force Camouflaged B-26s reached North Africa in late 1942 in the hands of the 319th BG, to be followed by the 320th and 17th Groups. To supplement the basic serial identification, small single letters were painted forward of the fuselage insignia and each aircraft was given a coloured rear fuselage band to distinguish its parent group — red for the 17th, white for the 319th and yellow for the 320th. The 319th also decorated the engine cowling lips in squadron colours — yellow for the 439th, white for the 440th, red for the 437th and green or blue for the 438th.

Two digit battle numbers were allocated to each B-26 group in late 1943 — 01-25 for the first squadron; 26-50, second; 51-75, third and 76-99 for the fourth. Initially white, these numbers were painted on the fin and rudder, either under or over the serial, according to group preference. The 320th used its group colour for the numbers and many aircraft also had propeller bosses and mainwheel cover plates in yellow. A distinctive sharkmouth identified the B-26s of the 320th's 444th BS throughout hostilities.

On NMF aircraft, these markings

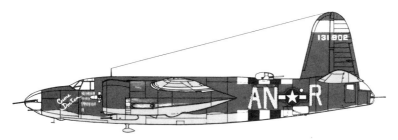

Martin B-26B Marauder 41-31902 of the 553rd BS, 386th BG, 9th Air Force. OD and Neutral Grey camouflage with yellow group tail band and serial, grey codes.

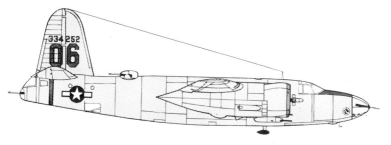

Martin B-26G Marauder 43-34252 of the 437th BS, 320th BG, 12th Air Force. Overall NMF with black serial and outline to plane-in-squadron battle number and squadron band. Yellow number, band and engine cowling front. OD antiglare panel.

changed little, apart from outlining to make them more visible.

8th and 9th Air Forces Camouflaged B-26s assigned to the 8th AF were camouflaged and had Sea Grey code letters painted on soon after their arrival. A good deal of juggling was necessary with the codes, due to limited space on the fuselage and the need to avoid compromising their 'readability' by having hatches and windows intrude into them. Even with Type 2 insignia it was a tight squeeze and when bars were added, the insignia was moved forward by three of the four groups.

Formation of B-26s of the 391st BG, 9th AF, with the aircraft on the left showing well the Medium Green blotching of wing and tailplane surfaces.

When transferred to the 9th AF, the B-26s were given tail markings — white horizontal fin/rudder band for the 323rd BG, and yellow bands for the 386th and the 387th, the latter's with six horizontal black stripes over it. The

A sharkmouthed B-26B 42-43304, number 95 of the 444th BS, 320th BG, 12th AF. Yellow group rear fuselage band and battle numbers.

USAAF camouflage of World War 2

A pair of B-26Cs of the 454th BS, 323rd BG, 9th AF showing the varying treatment of the white group band on different finishes. The nearest aircraft, 42-107614/RJ-H, has it outlined in black on NMF, while that of 41-35352/S is straight on to OD. Both machines have over-painted AEAF stripes.

322nd had no tail markings.

Similar ID markings were stipulated for the four new B-26 groups of the 9th — a white fin triangle for the 344th, a yellow triangle for the 391st, a diagonal white band for the 394th and a diagonal yellow band for the 397th. On NMF, yellow and white markings were edged in black. Code letters remained in Sea Grey in most cases, but some units had aircraft with their codes outlined in black on OD finish.

After the abandonment of camouflage, many Marauders re-adopted upper surface paintwork as tactical camouflage. In most cases, the wings and vertical and horizontal tailplanes were painted, as well as the fuselage upper decking, usually following a line from the lower edge of the cockpit windows, through the wing root to the tailplane leading edge. British paints were widely used, often with a greener cast than Olive Drab.

When AEAF stripes were applied to Marauders, the area encompassing the national insignia and codes was generally masked off, both top and bottom stripes ending in straight lines. 'Removal' of the black and white stripes was usually effected by an overspray of green or OD, even on NMF machines, especially where non-washable paint had been used.

For night missions, some Marauders of the 323rd BG were repainted black overall, with white code letters and standard yellow serials.

North American B-25 Mitchell

5th Air Force Few unit markings were employed by B-25C and D models used by the 3rd Bomb Group from April 1942, apart from serial numbers, which were set lower than usual on fins/rudders. Some of the group's B-25Cs were ex-Dutch contract machines and had larger than standard fuselage insignia.

September 1942 saw the 71st and 405th Squadrons of the 38th BG enter combat with camouflaged B-25s, again with only serials to identify them. By late 1943 however, the 405th was using striking 'green dragon' paintwork on the noses of some aircraft, the device being based on the squadron emblem. The 71st and 823rd Squadrons also used 'beast head' designs, a wolf for the former and a tiger for the latter. The fourth squadron of the group, the 822nd, did not apparently use a nose design.

In addition to nose markings, sections of the vertical tail surfaces were painted in squadron colours — yellow portion above the top hinge for the 71st, and yellow, Sky Blue and green for the 822nd, 823rd and 405th respec-

tively, the colour being on the lower section of the fin/rudder.

Prior to re-equipping with Liberators, the 2nd, 33rd and 408th Squadrons of the 22nd BG used camouflaged B-25s. One is known to have used white plane-in-squadron rudder letters and the 2nd BS applied a broad white horizontal fin band, upon which was a diamond-shaped emblem in black outline, with a flying bird design within it.

The famous 345th BG, the 'Air Apaches', entered combat with B-25Ds in June 1943, comprising the 498th 'Falcons', 499th 'Bats Outa Hell', 500th 'Rough Raiders' and 501st 'Black Panthers' squadrons.

Initially, stylised designs reflecting the squadron names were painted on the noses of the Mitchells — a yellow and green falcon's head for the 498th, a Medium Blue and white bat face for the 499th and a black panther's head for the 501st. The 500th applied its snorting mustang insignia to the fin/rudder on a white outlined blue disc. In line with these markings, the squadrons employed white airframe bands and trim. In squadron numerical order, these were — cowl rings; lower fin/rudder sections; fuselage

Striking nose decor of a B-25J of the 345th BG 'Air Apaches', 5th AF. This 'Bat Face' design was applied to many 499th BS aircraft, the colours being mainly blue with red and white detail.

bands aft of the wing; and chordwise mid-point fin/rudder bands respectively. Some 498th Squadron aircraft had all-white tails for a limited period.

From July 1944, the 345th applied an Apache Indian head group insignia to the tails of all squadron aircraft and each adopted coloured cowl rings — yellow, blue, red and orange-yellow respectively in numerical order. Those squadrons that had had white tail markings repositioned them: the 498th added white wingtips and the 501st chordwise wing bands.

The Indian head marking took various forms; the design was predominantly red, white and black and usually had a white circle surrounding a coloured disc or as an outline, the background being OD. Most aircraft had the last three digits of the overpainted serial repainted above the Apache insignia, which was carried over to a number of NMF aircraft used by the group.

USAAF camouflage of World War 2

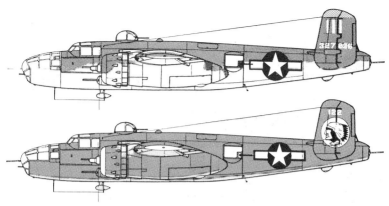

Top *North American B-25J Mitchell 43-27636 of the 447th BS, 321st BG, 12th Air Force. NMF with Olive Drab upper surfaces. White Roman numeral 'III' indicating squadron in group, with yellow serial below. Upper tip of fin/rudder in group colour, red.* **Above** *North American B-25J of the 498th BS, 345th BG, 5th Air Force. OD and NG camouflage, with white wingtips and cowl band. Last three digits of serial in yellow above 'Air Apaches' insignia.*

Camouflaged Mitchells of various models were flown by the 17th TRS, the early markings of which were a white lower band on the fin/rudder with a white vertical band against the hinge line. Later in the war, the squadron emblem, a comic aviator riding a bomb, appeared on the fins of some machines.

7th Air Force The 7th included the B-25-equipped 41st BG in its inventory, the aircraft of which were identified by serials. No other means of identity is known although the group had a number of machines with Medium Green splotching on upper surfaces — a common feature of Pacific-based Mitchells.

9th and 12th Air Forces First of the four B-25 groups in the MTO was the 12th, equipped with B-25Cs. Most early aircraft wore Sand and upper surface Sea Grey/Azure Blue underside finish and white battle numbers identified the squadrons — 1-25 for the 81st, 26-50 for the 82nd, 51-75 for the 83rd and 76-99 for the 434th. These digits appeared on both fins and rudders and were 36 inches (91.44 cm) high before application of the RAF fin flash theatre marking and 24 inches (60.96 cm) thereafter. The

numbers were usually re-positioned above the flash and, in many cases, over the serial, which was in turn repainted black, although not in every case.

Some machines of the 12th and other Mitchell groups had national insignia on both wing upper surfaces.

The 340th BG used both Sand and camouflaged machines, Sand being applied over OD or as shadow shading. Occasionally British Dark Green was used, but in general, replacement aircraft remained in standard OD and NG. To distinguish its aircraft from those of the 12th BG, the 340th used a plane-in-squadron letter, preceded by the last digit of the squadron number — these being the 498th, 487th, 488th and 489th. Letter/number combinations were painted on the fin and rudder in white in similar dimensions to those of the 12th BG. The 340th's B-25s tended to have serials repainted in black when the RAF fin flash obscured the original yellow digits.

The two Mitchell units assigned directly to the 12th AF were the 310th and 321st, which used coloured tail bands as their group identification markings. Upon arrival in the theatre,

Formation of B-25Cs of the 82nd BS, 12th BG, 12th AF. The nearest machine, 41-12863, has Sand and Azure Blue finish and white battle numbers.

Formation of Mitchells of the 489th BS, 340th BG, with a solitary Olive Drab machine from the 12th BG at upper right. Various finishes are displayed by these B-25Cs, which are coded 9T, H, A, Z and B. One aircraft has two upper wing insignia and all show evidence of much retouching and overpainting.

the aircraft of the 310th had the US flag on their outer fins, which soon gave way to a yellow horizontal group band at varying locations. Coloured propeller bosses identified the squadrons — white for the 379th, light blue for the 380th, yellow for the 381st and red for the 428th. In 1944, these colours were also added to the tail band as a second band, divided by a thin black band.

A red fin/rudder tip was applied to the 321st BG's B-25s, usually taking up the area above the top rudder hinge line. In late 1943, each squadron adopted a Roman numeral to identify it — I for the 445th, II for the 446th, III for the 447th and IV for the 448th. These numerals were placed on the fin/rudder in white, a shade that remained in general use even when the group received NMF B-25Js, as many were given an upper surface coat of OD, Medium or Dark Green as tactical camouflage. In some cases, the undersides were resprayed in grey. The demarcation line of the upper surface green varied greatly between aircraft throughout the group. Roman identification numerals gave way to

USAAF camouflage of World War 2

Arabic numbers in late 1944, prior to the 321st's return to the US.

Tactical camouflage was also widely used by the 340th BG, although ID markings were sometimes in black, application varying considerably between the squadrons. The 301st Group made little use of tactical paintwork on NMF B-25Js, the coloured tail bands being highlighted by black edging bands.

A fifth group, the 319th, flew B-25s for little more than a month before returning to the US to re-equip with Invaders. Both OD and NMF B-25s were used, with white Arabic tail numbers on both OD and NMF aircraft, as the entire vertical tailplane was painted black. Serials on the latter shade were left on a NMF patch.

10th Air Force When the 12th BG transferred from the MTO to the CBI theatre, it continued to use tail battle number identification on B-25G, H and J models. Many solid gun nose examples sported 'beast face' designs in various colours. Known tail numbers indicate that these markings were used by the group in general rather than particular squadrons; later in the war — probably 1945 — the 12th is believed to have adopted coloured rudders and cowl rings on some aircraft.

The 341st BG, known as the 'Burma

B-25H of the 1st Air Commando Group, showing the unmistakable white fuselage stripes. The machine is 43-4329, numbered 2.

Bridge Busters', flew a variety of Mitchells, entering combat early in 1943. Its aicraft carried no large ID markings, although it was common practice in the group to paint out the tail serial and re-apply the last three digits as plane-in-squadron numbers above the original position, in a more contrasting shade — ie white instead of yellow on OD. It was not unusual for machines of the group's 490th BS — and probably other squadrons — to paint unofficial badges on the forward nose; in the case of the 490th, the emblem was a white winged skull on a black disc surrounded by a white circle. For identification of individual aircraft on the flight line, a two-digit number was painted on the nosewheel hub cover plate. At least one aircraft of the group had a sharkmouth personal marking.

In 1944, the 341st Group absorbed the US element of the Chinese-American Provisional Group, which flew Mitchells in both American and Chinese Nationalist insignia. Few other markings were carried by the CAPG, but when the Chinese blue and white rudder stripes obscured some digits of the serial number on that surface, the 'last three' were repainted at the very top of the fin in black.

1st Air Commando Group The Mitchell was the only medium bomber operated by the Air Commandoes, the majority being B-25H models with nose-mounted 75 mm cannon. OD and NG-finished machines carried factory-applied yellow tail serials and

small black identification numbers on the nose, forward of the rectangular armour plate under the cockpit. In many cases, this plate was a field modification and partly covered existing nose art and names, at least until there was time for a respray. Air Commando Mitchells were identified by five white diagonal fuselage stripes on camouflage finish and black on NMF.

11th Air Force B-25B, C and D models of the 77th BS, operating as part of the 28th Composite Group in the Aleutians, were in OD and NG, with serial identification. The last two or three digits were repeated, often in 'stencil' style, below the canopy on each side of the fuselage in large light grey or white characters. Red outline national insignia was used with such markings in late 1943.

13th Air Force Most Mitchell models were used by the 42nd Bomb Group, which had five squadrons assigned to it during the later war years. Early aircraft were in OD and NG with standard yellow serials, but in the spring of 1943, the group applied a light grey shield to the outer vertical tail surfaces. Upon the shield was a red cross device, with two horizontal arms, angled downwards at each side of a vertical arm. Squadron colours are believed to have been applied to the fin/rudder tips. A distinctive feature of the 42nd's B-25s — including J models — was that both OD and NMF aircraft had *two* serials on each vertical tail surface. Due to the shield marking bisecting the original factory number, it was deemed necessary to repaint the serial on the extreme lower face of the fin/rudder in larger size than the original.

De Havilland Mosquito

Approximately 160 Mosquitoes were allocated to the USAAF, variants including the B VI Srs II, T III, PR XVI and NF 30 from UK stocks and Mks XX and VII from Canada, the majority of the latter being modified for PR work under the designation F-8.

8th Air Force Following the use of some Mk VIIs in the KB serial range by the 375th Servicing Squadron, the main 8th AF Mosquito variants were Mk XVIs finished in PRU Blue with USAAF insignia in standard positions and Roundel Blue spinners. Aircraft were identified by RAF serials and individual code letters and were used by the 802nd Recon Group (Provisional), the 8th Recon Squadron and the 8th Weather Squadron, Light. To distinguish the weather squadron machines, their white fin letters were given a white circle outline. On August 16 1944, all 8th AF Mosquitoes had red vertical tail surfaces as an added recognition feature.

PRU Blue was left as a background circle to the ID letters of the 653rd BS, which the 8th WRS became in 1944. The white circle was soon removed, however, and red was extended to the entire tail unit, being brought forward

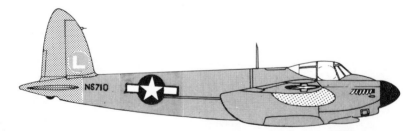

De Havilland Mosquito Mk XVI NS710 of the 653rd BS, 25th BG, 8th Air Force. Overall PRU Blue with red tail unit. Black serial and aircraft letter in white on PRU Blue fin circle. Insignia Blue spinners with NMF wing tanks.

on the fuselage to a point just short of the serial letters. The ID letter was painted directly on to the fin of most replacement machines of the 653rd.

AEAF stripes were applied to USAAF Mosquitoes and as their external wing tanks were centred on the outermost black stripe, they were usually painted in that shade, but were otherwise blue or NMF.

Black was applied to the under surfaces of some 654th BS aircraft in late 1944-45 for special reconnaissance duties, the shade being gloss Jet Black. Some machines carried names and an operational record on the nose, and the 654th recorded missions in the form of tiny red lightning flashes and white clouds — an abbreviated form of the squadron emblem. Night flash photo sorties were shown as a camera above a falling bomb.

The few Mk III trainers used are believed to have retained standard RAF markings.

12th Air Force One of the first Mossies in US markings to see combat was a single Mk IV of the 5th Recon Group operating out of Algiers during mid-1943. Earlier, one or two examples of five Mk VIIIs — KB312, 313, 315, 316 and 317 — allocated the US serials 43-34924-5 and 43-34926-8 respectively, are believed to have flown a number of missions in the Middle East, probably in the hands of the 3rd PRS in Algeria. Some Mosquitoes were also on the strength of the 32nd PRS of the 5th PRG in 1944.

RAF camouflage and markings are believed to have been retained by the ten Mk 30s night fighters flown by the elements of the 416th and 425th Squadrons from Pisa in 1944.

P-51 Mustang

5th Air Force Black and white fuselage and wing theatre bands were applied to NMF P-51Ds of the 35th FG, squadrons being identified by col-

North American P-51B, 42-106950 of the 354th FS, 355th FG, 8th AF. The mount of ace F. R. Haviland on several occasions, the aircraft was named the 'Iowa Beaut' and had white recognition markings and OD upper surfaces for post-invasion operations.

oured spinners and nose bands — light blue for the 39th FS, red for the 40th and yellow for the 41st. The band was often swept back in a blaze and outlined in black. Aircraft numbers were in blocks of around 30 for each squadron, and were painted on the fin between two horizontal black bands and were in black or squadron colours. Rudder stripes were also used at the war's end.

The 348th FG's markings were similar to those used on P-47s; all P-51Ds

were NMF and squadrons had coloured vertical fin bands — yellow, red, blue and black for the 340th, 341st, 242nd and 460th respectively. Aircraft numbers were 1-25, 26-50, 51-75 and 100-139, applied to the band in black/white. Theatre bands and rudder stripes were widely used and spinners were in squadron colours, black or white.

F-6D/K Mustangs of the 82nd and 110th TacRecon Squadrons of the 71st TRG were numbered 40-69 and 10-39 respectively; theatre bands were applied and spinner cones and tail tips were white for the 110th and yellow for the 82nd, edged in black. Numbers were on both fin/rudder, in white or squadron colours, often with black shadows. Spinners were in squadron colours.

3rd Air Commando Group NMF P-51Ds had wing and fuselage theatre bands and dark blue fin/rudder bands, with a yellow letter or number. Spinners were in various patterns, often with a sweptback nose blaze, in squadron colours — light blue for the 3rd FS, red for the 4th.

7th and 20th Air Forces The 15th, 21st and 506th Groups used P-51Ds, the first two groups being part of VII Fighter Command, the 506th coming within the jurisdiction of the 20th. All aircraft were NMF, aircraft of the 15th FG's squadrons having green diagonal wing and tailplane bands, edged black for the 45th FS; chordwise main and tailplane and fuselage bands

in black, edged yellow for the 47th, which also had a triangular fin/rudder section in black and yellow; and yellow and black wing, tailplane, fin and rudder tips for the 78th.

Black numbers indicated squadrons — 51-99, 150-199 and 100-149 — with spinner colours in black/green/NMF; yellow/black/yellow and yellow/black respectively. Squadron badges were carried by some 45th and 78th FS aircraft.

Black wing and tailplane tips and fin/rudder bands identified the 21st FG — blue for the 46th FS, yellow for the 72nd and white for the 531st, numbers being in the 100, 200 and 300 ranges respectively. Spinners were usually in squadron colours, with black nose bands.

The 506th FG painted the fixed tail sections of its P-51Ds red (457th FS), diagonal black stripes (458th) and yellow (462nd), with numbers 500-549, 550-599 and 600-649.

8th Air Force Camouflaged P-51A and B models coded AX were first in the UK, being used by the 107th TRG. These early machines had rear fuselage serials, which were repainted on the fin/rudder.

P-51Bs of the 354th FG received the white type recognition bands stipu-

Nice shot of a 363rd FS P-51D 44-13573, named 'Isabel II'. Two kills in the form of black German crosses appear under the windshield (T. Bennett).

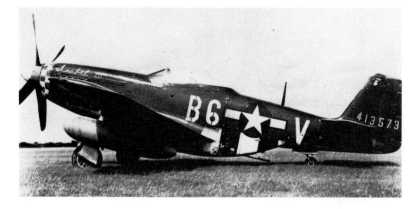

USAAF camouflage of World War 2

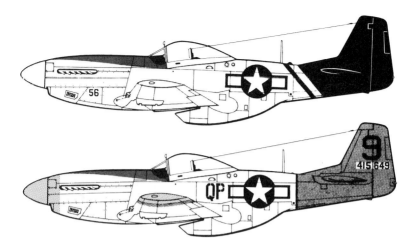

Top *North American P-51K Mustang of the 75th FS, 23rd FG, 14th AF. Overall NMF with tail unit and aircraft number in black. The aircraft was the same on the reverse side, but with the squadron emblem, a blue and white flying tiger shark on a black disc, forward of the national insignia.* **Above** *North American P-51D 44-15649 of the 2nd FS, 52nd FG, 15th AF. Overall NMF with yellow tailplane and wingtip bands inboard of red tips. Red spinner and nose band, black codes and serial.*

lated for all ETO P-51s to avoid confusion with the Bf 109 — on spinner, nose, wing, tailplane and fin/rudder.

From the spring of 1944, the 8th AF's fighter groups used coloured nose and tail markings, each of the three wings adopting different basic patterns — groups of the 65th FW, nose band and red, yellow and blue rudders; the 66th, spinner bands and nose checks and black, white, yellow, red and green rudders and the 67th, yellow, red and blue rudders and various nose markings — black and white vertical bars for the 20th FG, upswept blue for the 352nd, downswept green for the 359th, horizontal blue diamonds on red for the 364th and horizontal white and blue stripes for the 364th. The 20th and 364th also retained their square, triangle and circle ID markings.

9th Air Force General finish and codes were similar to those of the 8th AF, colour markings being used mainly after the 9th went to France. Early markings were applied over rec-

ognition bands by the 354th FG — blue spinners and nose checks for the 355th FS, blue triangles for the 353rd and white stars on a blue nose band for the 356th. In 1945, yellow, blue and red spinners and nose bands were used by the three squadrons.

Red, yellow and blue nose bands/spinners identified the 380th, 381st and 382nd Squadrons of the 363rd FG, some P-51Bs having OD upper surfaces over NMF.

The 370th Group had yellow, blue and red nose markings and horizontal, vertical and diagonal tail stripes for the 401st, 402nd and 485th Squadrons.

Reconnaissance Mustangs of the 9th used a variety of colour trim, on rudder tabs, noses and tails, although code letters continued to be the most reliable form of identification. In 1945, the 10th and 22nd Squadrons had their aircraft's NMF rudders quartered in red and green and the 11th TRS used narrow green diagonal tail stripes. Medium blue/white tail checks identified the 10th PRG, with red, yellow and blue spinners and nose checks for the 162nd, 12th and 15th Squadrons respectively.

10th and 14th Air Forces P-51B/Cs of the 23rd FG continued to use the AVG sharkmouth, although their identification details are sketchy. Aircraft with two white and yellow horizontal tail bands were probably part of the group and one squadron is thought to have had fin numbers without the bands.

Later markings were a black Indian head on fin/rudder for the 74th FS, black tail with diagonal band for the 75th FS and black nose paint swept back to the cockpit for the 76th. Numbers identified all squadrons — presentation being on the fin in all cases, the 75th moving them to the nose when black tails were applied.

On attachment to the 23rd FG, the 118th TRS used F-6C/D and P-51Ds in NMF with a spinner-to-tailplane black lightning flash, edged in yellow, with a second flash on the vertical tail. Spinners were black, white and yellow in various patterns and three-digit tail numbers identified each machine.

Initially using A-36s and P-51As, the 311th FBG used rear fuselage serials to identify its aircraft, later introducing fin numbers and letters and possibly, nose bands in squadron colours. On NMF P-51Ds, all-yellow tailplanes had two vertical, two horizontal black stripes to indicate the 529th and 530th Squadrons respectively. Four-digit numbers were painted below the cockpit.

1st Air Commando Group The group entered combat with camouflaged P-51As marked with five diagonal white fuselage stripes, which obscured yellow serials. Some aircraft also had fin/rudder stripes. Coloured tail tips and small white rudder numbers identified aircraft within the group, which had the 5th and 6th Fighter Squadrons assigned. One of them (flying P-51B/Cs) is believed to have used diagonal-pattern fin/rudder checks, and both checks and diagonal stripes were seen on P-51s at the end of the war.

2nd Air Commando Group NMF P-51Ds were used by the 1st and 2nd Squadrons of the 2nd ACG, marked with fin/rudder and mid-point wing and tailplane black bands. The fin part of the tail band was bisected by the group marking, an exclamation mark.

A NMF P-51D, 'Love of Mine' of the 363rd FS, 357th FG, 8th AF. The broken line of the OD anti-glare panel suggests that a replacement was taken from another aircraft (T. Bennett).

USAAF camouflage of World War 2

Row upon row of Mustangs of the 21st FG, 7th AF, on Iwo Jima in 1945. The nearest aircraft have the white and black edged bands of the 531st FS and 'stencil' style numbers.

Both squadrons embellished these basic markings with black diagonal lightning bolts, angled out from the bands on the leading edges of all wing and tailplane surfaces. A further bolt was painted from the cockpit to the rear fuselage. Spinners were in various designs of black, white or colours. Two-digit black nose numbers and serials identified individual aircraft.

12th and 15th Air Forces A-36s of the 27th and 86th Fighter Bomber Groups initially had yellow rear fuselage serials on OD finish and yellow theatre wing bands.

The 27th Group applied a white fin/rudder letter to identify its squadrons — A for the 524th, B for the 522nd and C for the 523rd — underneath which was an ID letter. Spinners were in squadron colours — red, blue and white respectively.

The 86th Group used a white diagonal fin/rudder stripe and the letter A for its 527th Squadron aircraft and B and C were probably used for the 525th and 526th Squadrons, although this is unconfirmed. Letters were applied to the fuselage, that for

the squadron forward of the insignia, that for the aircraft aft, often over the serial.

The 111th and 154th TR Squadrons also used camouflaged P-51s marked with yellow theatre bands and initially, the US flag across fin/rudder. Machines of the former unit had two letter codes aft of the fuselage insignia, the first indicating A, B or C Flights, the second the aircraft. Codes usually obscured serials until the 111th moved to Europe, where these were repainted on the fin/rudder.

The fighter groups of the 15th AF used both letter codes and numbers — MX, HL and WZ for the 307th, 308th and 309th Squadrons of the 31st FG and VF, WD and QP for the 5th, 4th and 2nd Squadrons of the 52nd FG. Most 31st Group Mustangs were in NMF, initially having a single red diagonal tail stripe. Later, the group painted stripes on all tail surfaces. Codes were black and, late in the war, some machines had an ID number.

The 52nd FG applied the squadron codes to the fuselage and the ID letter to the tail. Codes were usually black on the fuselage and yellow on the tail, sometimes outlined in black. A broad yellow rear fuselage band led to all-yellow tail units in the group and the letter of the flight to which a particular aircraft was assigned was often painted in white on a small red rectangle aft of the cockpit on P-51B and C models.

Red spinners and wingtips became theatre markings for 15th AF P-51s and these markings were elaborated upon by the 325th FG, the 'Checkertails'. This group painted a yellow band inboard of the red wingtip as well as black/yellow tail checks — eventually on all tail surfaces, apart from a NMF strip at the tailplane root.

The 325th's squadrons were identified by numbers — 10-39 for the 317th FS, 40-69 for the 318th and 70-99 for the 319th. Numbers out of those sequences — eg 100, 00 — were used by flight commanders. Where a number duplicated, an A prefix was applied.

Mustangs of the 322nd FG had

theatre markings and all-red tailplanes with a diagonal demarcation line on the fuselage. Each of the four squadrons was identified by coloured trim tabs and nose bands — white/red and white checkerboard in diamond pattern for the 99th FS; black/red band for the 100th; blue/yellow and red horizontal stripes for the 301st; and yellow — possibly blue — and red nose band for the 302nd.

The 99th FS had A prefix numbers, which were split by the national insignia.

Douglas C-47 Skytrain

5th Air Force Standard Olive Drab and grey finish was used on most wartime C-47s and the 5th AF's 54th Troop Carrier Group and 2nd Combat Cargo Group identified their machines by white, yellow or light grey numerals behind the cockpit — 1-99 for the 374th TCG, 100-199 for the 375th, probably also 1-99 for the 317th and

Low over the sea during the 12th AF build-up in North Africa is C-47 41-18376, 'Miss Carriage'. The photograph bears evidence of either the censor's brush or unit overpainting of the aircraft code, which may have identified it as a machine of the 12th AF's 60th or 64th Troop Carrier Groups.

C-47s of the 83rd (code T2), 76th (CW) and 77th (IB) Troop Carrier Squadrons during the invasion period. The 83rd was part of the 9th AF's 437th TCG, the other two of the 435th. Various camouflage finishes can be seen in the line-up and the second aircraft is believed to be 41-100578, a C-47A.

USAAF camouflage of World War 2

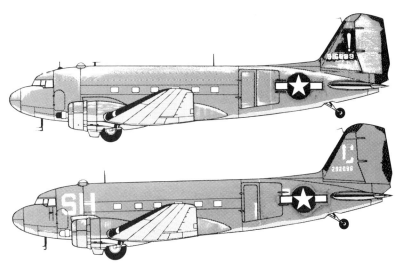

Top *Douglas C-47A 43-15699 of the 2nd Air Commando Group, 14th AF. Overall OD and NG finish with yellow serial and white group exclamation mark on fin. Very weathered finish had Medium Green blotching on rudder.* **Above** *Douglas C-47A 42-92098 of the 75th Troop Carrier Squadron, 435th TCG, 9th Air Force. Overall OD and grey finish with faded light grey squadron codes aft of cockpit. Yellow serial. The aircraft had traces of AEAF stripes on the fuselage and Medium Green blotches on the tail unit.*

300-399 for the 433rd. Aircraft of the 317th added an X prefix to the number and the name 'Jungle Skippers' was often painted above the cabin windows in yellow or white. Medium Green blotching was applied to many C-47s in the Pacific theatres.

8th and 9th Air Forces ETO C-47s had little identification other than serials and single plane-in-squadron letters prior to the invasion, letters being white or light grey.

For D-Day, IX Troop Carrier Command C-47s were given two letter/letter-number squadron codes, which were presented aft of the cockpit in white, light grey or yellow, with the aircraft letter on the fin above the serial. AEAF stripes were applied to fuselage and wings, 'removal' often being by a coat of OD or other green paint. It was common for Skytrains to have their mission records above the cabin windows, often on a black panel.

10th and 14th Air Forces Yellow or black serials identified CBI transports in most cases, although squadrons

used both letters and numerals to identify individual aircraft. Trim tabs were also painted and aircraft numbers were presented on the rudder, which was in turn in a contrasting shade. In one case, the letter A identified the unit, with the aircraft letter grouped with it on the rudder — AA, AB, AC and so on. Two examples in Burma in 1944 were C-47As 42-100686/AB and 42-100681/A2, each code being in white on the rudder. The latter machine had the number repeated aft of the cockpit in black.

1st Air Commando Group Camouflaged C-47s had five diagonal white fuselage stripes along with the unit marking, a black question mark, on the fin. Black serials were common.

2nd Air Commando Group The group's marking was an exclamation mark, which was carried by some camouflaged C-47s on the fin in white, above the serial.

12th and 15th Air Forces Numbers and letters were used by C-47 units in the MTO, often both. For Operation

Douglas C-47 Skytrain

45

Torch, camouflaged Skytrains had yellow national insignia surrounds and RAF theatre fin flashes. USAAF aircraft flying into Morocco had the US flag on their fins and rudders and machines of the 60th and 64th Groups had single yellow/light grey letters aft of the national insignia.

C-47s of the Air Transport Command carried the ATC badge on the fuselage, usually adjacent to the national insignia.

Supermarine Spitfire

8th Air Force The first application of the US star marking to Spitfires was by the 31st and 52nd Fighter Groups, which arrived in the UK during the summer of 1942. Along with a few Mk IIa and Va aircraft for training, the main combat variant was the Mk Vb in standard RAF Ocean Grey and Dark Green camouflage with Medium Sea Grey undersides. Sky rear fuselage bands were retained at first, as were Sky spinners and yellow wing leading edge stripes. When US insignia was applied, the upper starboard and lower port wing roundels were overpainted.

The Type C1 and A1 fuselage roundels were obscured completely in many cases, although the outer ring of the RAF marking was left in others, as the 32 inch (86.36 cm) diameter of the US star disc corresponded to the outer blue rim of the roundel. Most aircraft that had the yellow surround left on had had them removed by September 1942, a month or so before the directive to add a yellow surround to US markings as an aid to recognition. Both the 31st and 52nd Groups had little time to comply however, as they sailed for North Africa in November.

In the 31st Group it was common to repeat the serial near the top of the fin in four inch (10.16 cm) high characters to conform to American practice of presenting identification numbers on vertical tail surfaces.

While under RAF control in the UK, American fighter units were issued with three letter codes, which were painted on Spitfires in Sky, with stencil breaks left unpainted, at least for a time, on some examples.

When the Eagle squadrons were absorbed by the 4th Fighter Group in September 1942, their Spitfires retained the same RAF codes until the 4th adopted new letters.

Some confusion may have arisen after the 31st and 52nd Groups left England as many of their aircraft were

Spitfire Mk V, EN851/D named 'Lima Challenger'. The serial appears at the top of the fin of this 307th FS machine, in accordance with US practice of presenting aircraft identification on the vertical tail surfaces. The characters 'CBAF/2886' appear on the rudder tip. Seen at Merston in August 1942, the machine has standard RAF camouflage and was part of the 31st FG at that time.

USAAF camouflage of World War 2

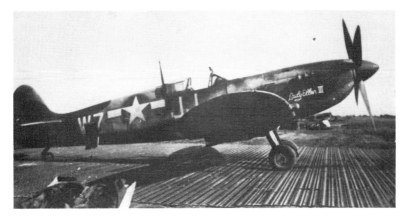

Spitfire Mk IX, WZ-JJ of the 309th FS, 31st FG, pictured in Italy. Red spinner and outline to national insignia, white 'Lady Ellen III'. Use of two ID codes when a letter duplicated was common in this group.

used by the 67th Observation Group without being repainted. The codes ZM, AX and VX were allocated to the 12th, 107th and 109th Observation Squadrons respectively, the fourth unit, the 153rd OS, apparently not adopting codes. Red and yellow spinners were used by the 67th's machines in spring 1943.

Introduction of white bars to the national insignia meant that many Spitfires were repainted to position the codes and Sky band to avoid confusing overpainting. Most squadrons of the 67th did so, the exception being the 109th RS, which omitted the band.

At least eight Spitfire Mk XIs were used to boost the 8th AF's reconnaissance capacity during the war, operated by the 14th PS in standard RAF PRU blue overall with Roundel Blue spinners. The serial was repeated on the fin/rudder in yellow. By early 1945,

14th FG Spits were in NMF, with rudders in black, red or OD, with yellow or black serials, depending on background. Anti-glare panels were either OD or PRU Blue.

12th Air Force Tropicalised Spitfire Mk Vc models were used by the 31st and 52nd Groups in North Africa, finished in the RAF desert scheme of Dark Earth and Mid-Stone with Azure Blue undersides. Both groups continued to use their codes, which were initially in Sky or light grey and later white. The individual aircraft letter invariably obscured the serial and all letters of the alphabet were used. Where a letter duplicated, a second would be painted directly next to it. Aircraft letters were often repeated under the spinner in yellow and occasionally the pilot's initials would appear in that position. Spinners were mainly in red, the theatre colour for USAAF fighters.

These markings generally applied to Mk VIIIs and IXs, the former being used by the 31st FG, although a few Mk IXs were used in Italy in Dark Green and Ocean Grey camouflage with Medium Sea Grey below.

Boeing B-29 Superfortress

20th Air Force The B-29 was used by five Very Heavy Bomb Wings of the 20th AF and the 509th Composite Group, charged with the atomic bomb strikes. Initially, each of the four

groups within a wing had four squadrons, but this number was cut to three in 1944.

Early production B-29s were in OD and NG and some were used on operations, particularly by the 58th BW.

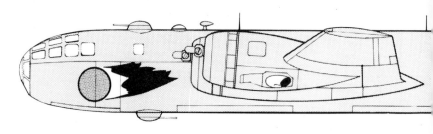

Boeing B-29 Superfortress of the 484th BS, 505th BG, 313th BW, 20th AF. Overall NMF with green tail tip and black / yellow / black lead crew stripe. Black aircraft number, wing symbol and group letter. Colours of nose emblem were probably yellow disc with red outline and white/black flash.

Boeing B-29 42-63394 of the 25th BS, 40th BG in January 1945. 'Last Resort' was badly damaged when the bombs of a sister aircraft exploded. Red tail stripes, black serial and aircraft letter (USAF).

Most Superfortresses mounting the early strikes from the CBI theatre had few markings apart from serials, black on NMF, white or yellow on camouflage.

The 58th BW was the first to fly missions and to facilitate identification, each group used a fin marking adjacent to the serial, the actual position further indicating the group — the 40th BG used an aircraft letter above the serial, the 444th numbers below, the 462nd letters above and the 463rd

the last three digits of the serial repeated above.

By August 1944, the 58th Wing's groups began to use coloured rudders. 40th BG — four horizontal fin/rudder bands in red, yellow, blue and black for the 25th, 44th, 45th and 395th Squadrons; 462nd BG — red, yellow, green and blue rudders for the 768th, 769th, 770th and 771st; and the 468th BG — two diagonal rudder bands, the colour of which identified squadrons — white, blue, red and yel-

USAAF camouflage of World War 2

Over half the striking power of the 29th BG can be seen here, with the Superforts bearing the 314th BW black square with group letter 'O'. At least four machines have black formation leader fin stripes.

low for the 792nd, 793rd, 794th and 795th. The 444th BG used a large white or black fin diamond above the serial, upon which was the aircraft-in-group number.

In October 1944, the 58th BW lost the fourth squadron in each group, whereupon the 462nd BG applied red rudders throughout, with a black number below the serial to identify the squadrons — 1 for the 768th, 2 for the 769th and 3 for the 770th.

The 444th BG also applied a new marking, in the form of a band in the squadron colour immediately forward of the fuselage observation blisters. Flight leaders' aircraft were identified by black diagonal stripes on the band and the 40th and 462nd Groups used black vertical dorsal fin bands for the same purpose.

After moving to the Marianas, the 58th BW's groups adopted a distinctive black triangle tail symbol, upon which was the group letter — S for the 40th, N for the 444th, U for the 462nd

The black tail markings identify this B-29 as a machine of the 499th BG, 73rd BW, 20th AF. The low numbers indicate the 887th BS and the machine has the factory 'hull number' K-253 on the forward fuselage. The last four digits of the serial are repainted on the fin.

and I for the 468th.

The groups of the 73rd BW were the first to adopt vertical letter-symbol-number fin markings, the letter indicating the group — A, T, V and Z for the 497th, 498th, 499th and 500th Squadrons respectively. A square indicated the 73rd Wing and the numbers 1-20, 21-40 and 41-60, the first, second and third squadrons. These markings were replaced by single letters without symbols. Markings similar to those of the 73rd BW were carried by the 313th Wing B-29s. The wing symbol was a triangle and group letters were L (later R), X, E and K (later W) for the 6th, 9th, 504th and 505th Groups respectively. Squadron numbers were in similar sequence to those of the 73rd Wing.

Later wing markings of the 313th were letters enclosed by a black circle, and colour markings were used by each group on fin/rudder tips and engine cowling panels — red, white, yellow and green respectively. Three groups also used black/yellow/black formation leader markings on the rear fuselage, although the 6th BG continued to use the abbreviated dorsal fin stripe.

The 314th BW used a square symbol, with the letters M, O, P and K for its 19th, 29th, 39th and 330th Groups; symbols and aircraft numbers were often repeated on engine cowlings.

A diamond was the symbol of the 315th BW, the letters B, H, L and Y identifying the 16th, 502nd, 331st and 501st Groups. Many aircraft had gloss black undersides for night operations.

Last Superfort group to see combat was the 509th Composite, which, to avoid any undue attention to its special mission, changed its arrowhead in a circle marking to those of other groups on Tinian. A dozen or so B-29s are believed to have used 'borrowed' markings, among them the 6th BG's Circle-R, the 39th's Square-P, the 444th's Triangle-N and the plain A of the 497th. Additionally, the 509th's aircraft were distinguished by numbers higher than those in general use by other groups — in the 70, 80 and 90 range. After the atomic strikes, the arrowhead tail markings were replaced.

A further B-29 unit was the 3rd Photographic Squadron. Its F-13As were marked with a black F on fin and fuselage nose, with serials retained.

USAAF camouflage of World War 2

P-47 Thunderbolt

5th Air Force From late 1943, the 8th FG's 36th Squadron flew camouflaged razorback P-47Ds, identified by single white cowling letters immediately followed by a small bird wing design, also in white. The letters were usually presented in italic style and cowl flaps were occasionally in white, as were tail units when theatre recognition markings were applied.

November 1943 saw the 35th FG convert to camouflaged P-47s, but a few NMF aircraft were soon being used. Theatre markings were applied and squadrons used coloured forward cowling rings to identify them — blue for the 39th, red for the 40th and yellow for the 41st, the bands often being outlined in black or white and swept back on either side in a blaze design.

Aircraft numbers appeared on the fin and the lower cowling lip, often in the squadron colour. Machines of the 40th FS also sported a diagonal red lightning flash across the fin/rudder above the serial, which was often left on an OD patch when white tail markings were added.

In the 35th Group, horizontal fin bands in the squadron colours were used in conjunction with theatre markings, and the aircraft ID number was painted on in a contrasting shade.

Colours were changed to light blue for the 39th FS and Insignia Blue for the 41st, the latter using yellow band numbers, the other squadrons white. In 1945, the 35th had the Mexican Air Force's 201 Escuadron attached to it, markings being similar to other squadrons in the group, with the addition of green/white /red rudder stripes and the triangular Mexican national insignia on upper starboard and lower port wings.

The 49th FG's 9th Squadron flew P-47s, all known examples being camouflaged. Numbers from 70-99 appeared aft of the cowling flaps, which were painted white on some machines; white theatre tail markings were also used.

Camouflaged razorback P-47Ds of the 58th FG also had theatre markings, although some aircraft did not have the upper surfaces of their tailplanes painted. Serials were generally left on OD patches and coloured cowlings identified squadrons — white for the 69th, yellow for the 310th and blue for the 311th; an alpha-numeric code indicated the squadron and aircraft — A1-33, H34-66 and V67-99 respectively. On NMF aircraft, cowl colours were reduced to an horizontal band, codes were black and rudder striping was applied to many examples. The 69th

Typical ETO theatre and squadron markings on P-47D 42-8369 of the 61st FS, 56th FG. The fuselage insignia shows the blue surround applied over the red surround after September 1943, and the codes still have stencil breaks.

Some idea of the diversity of 56th FG Thunderbolt colour schemes can be gleaned from this shot of eight 61st FS machines. Three tones of green and grey — probably blue as well — have been applied to HV-N, while others have basically two colour finish. All aircraft have red cowl rings and rudders.

FS changed its colour to red in late 1944.

When black/white theatre bands were applied, codes were often not repainted and were soon dropped altogether. Variations in the group's markings included the painting of alternate cowl flaps and aircraft with both old and revised cowl colours where this section of the machine had been transferred to a new arrival.

The 348th Group introduced the P-47 to the Pacific theatre, entering combat with camouflaged machines with white theatre markings, coloured tail tips identifying squadrons — yellow for the 340th, red for the 341st and blue for the 342nd. Aircraft numbers were 1-25, 26-50 and 51-75 respectively and were painted on the fin in black or the squadron colour and in small white characters on each side of the lower cowl ring. Serials were generally left on an OD tail patch.

By late 1944, NMF Thunderbolts of the group — by then joined by the 460th FS — carried vertical fin band markings in squadron colours, with white or black numbers, one over the other. Theatre bands and rudder striping was also carried.

7th Air Force The 318th FG used P-47D to N models and began operations with camouflaged machines, identified by lack of paint on the cowlings and all tail surfaces in the 19th Squadron. A single chordwise blue band on all tail surfaces further identified the 19th's P-47s all of which also had white aircraft letters aft of the cockpit.

The group's 73rd FS identified its machines by white bands of similar width and positioning to those of ETO Thunderbolts. In addition, a vertical fuselage band was applied immediately aft of the cockpit as well as white wingtips. Aircraft numbers, 1-37, were painted on the fuselage forward of the band. Numbers were repeated — not always in full — on the mainwheel plates. It is believed that the 33rd FS used markings similar to those of the 73rd, but in yellow and probably carried numbers in the 400 range. All markings mentioned applied to razorback P-47Ds.

NMF P-47Ns of the 318th Group had black and yellow tail markings — three diagonal black bands on all-yellow tail surfaces for the 19th FS, half black, half NMF tail surfaces with white air-

USAAF camouflage of World War 2

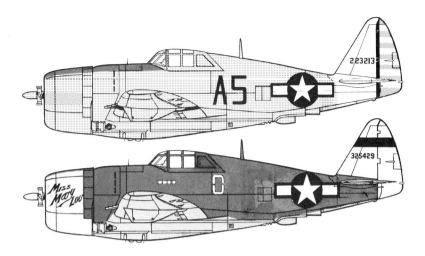

Top *Republic P-47D Thunderbolt 42-23213 of the 69th FS, 58th FG, 5th Air Force; overall NMF with white theatre markings on tail, with blue, white and red rudder stripes. Black aircraft code and serial. Red horizontal stripe on cowling. Black theatre wing bands. This aircraft carried the name 'Marge A Minnesota Maid' on the starboard cowl stripe.* **Above** *P-47D Thunderbolt 43-25429 of the 19th FS, 318th FG, 7th Air Force. Camouflage finish except for tailplane and cowling. Blue horizontal tail band and white plane-in-squadron letter, black name. OD anti-glare panel left on top of cowl.*

An aircraft of the 367th FS, 358th FG, 9th AF, P-47D 42-6436 well illustrates the short-lived full AEAF stripes.

craft numbers in the black area for the 73rd FS, and half yellow, half NMF tail surfaces for the 333rd, the yellow areas being trimmed with black.

8th Air Force Camouflaged P-47Cs were the first Thunderbolts in the UK, in early 1943. They were soon given the special white cowl ring, and tail surface bands to avoid confusion with the Fw 190, as well as larger-size national insignia under both wings. Fuselage roundels received the two inch (5.08 cm) yellow surround at the same time.

White squadron code letters were painted forward of the national insignia on both sides of the fuselage with the ID aircraft letter aft and these remained standard markings until February 1944, when the 56th FG applied red and yellow cowl ring colours for the 61st and 62nd Squadrons respectively. Thereafter, VIII Fighter Command P-47s began to display nose and rudder markings, with some units — but by no means all — paint-

P-47D 44-20465 of the 366th FS showing the later markings of the 358th FG when it transferred to the 1st Tactical Air Force in late 1944. The aircraft has the orange tail surfaces with the serial left on a NMF patch. The cowl ring was yellow.

ing out recognition bands on the fin and rudder, though those on the horizontal tailplanes endured until the end of the war in some cases, being repainted black on NMF.

Black and white AEAF stripes were removed from the top surfaces of Thunderbolts within a month of the Allied landings in France, but they tended to remain on undersides until the war's end on certain aircraft. Some groups, including the 78th, repainted the upper surfaces of NMF machines in green for tactical camouflage, the Duxford-based squadrons also including the undersides, which were resprayed in Sky, using British paints. But it was the 56th Group that employed the widest possible variations of upper surfaces camouflage and code letter presentation, schemes including shadow shading in green, grey, blue and overall black.

9th Air Force All but two of the 9th AF's Thunderbolt groups used letter/number codes, presented similarly to those of 8th AF units. Camouflaged and NMF aircraft markings also conformed to 8th practice, although colour markings were applied in a more random — and in many cases more extensive — fashion. The first 9th P-47 group to use colour trim was the

406th, which adopted red, yellow and blue cowl rings for the 513th, 512th and 514th Squadrons respectively.

Among the individualistic markings sported by other 9th AF P-47 groups was the application of the nickname 'Easy's Angels' above the horizontal fin/rudder band on aircraft of the 36th FG's 23rd FS, and bands of blue triangles, light blue diamonds and white stars encircling the cowlings of the 353rd, 355th and 356th Squadrons' aircraft in the 354th Group.

Most of these striking colour applications were to be seen on NMF P-47s, both razorback and bubble canopy models, although there were some camouflaged razorbacks on hand throughout 1944.

10th and 14th Air Forces The 5th and 6th Squadrons of the 1st Air Commando Group received razorback P-47s in 1944, most, if not all of which were in NMF. After a few early missions, each aircraft had five diagonal rear fuselage stripes applied in Insignia Blue or black, while cowl rings, wings and vertical and horizontal tailplanes were given black bands.

It appears that Commando plane-in-squadron markings took different forms in each squadron — one or two digit black fuselage numbers for the

5th and white numbers on the tailband for the 6th, both styles of marking being seen on razorback models.

A number of P-47D-30s in NMF carried Commando stripes at the end of the war, as well as wing and tail bands, one known example having a fuselage number and a single letter on the cowling.

Both the 33rd and 81st Groups used camouflaged razorbacks, the first being identified by a diagonally-forward sloping fin/rudder stripe carried through to the bottom of the fuselage and the 81st by a diagonally-rearward sloping stripe, which ended on the rudder. A horizontal tail band identified the 80th Group which, along with the 33rd, also applied cowl ring, wing and tailplane bands, white on OD and black on NMF. Number blocks identified squadrons within the groups, the 33rd being thought to have used digits in the 900 range, the others numbers up to 99. Incidentally, all razorback P-47s in the CBI had an upper decking D/F loop housing.

12th and 15th Air Forces Four of the eight P-47s groups in the MTO had converted from P-40s and their markings reflected those carried on the older type; whereas Warhawks had red spinners as theatre markings, the Thunderbolts invariably sported red cowl rings and individual aircraft were identified by numbers — 10-39, 40-69 and 70-99, low numbers for the lowest numbered squadron in the group and so on. All but two of the groups had three squadrons, exceptions being the 350th and 332nd.

In the 27th FG, a red, medium blue and yellow horizontal tail stripe identified the 522nd, 523rd and 524th Squadrons respectively and aircraft of the last two squadrons had single ID letters on the fin, the 522nd's being on the fuselage, in the squadron colour for the first two units, black for the third. Late in the war, some machines had ID numbers. Coloured alternate cowling flaps, wheel plates and prop bosses additionally identified squadrons in the 27th.

Red cowls were used by the 57th FG, with white battle numbers often shadowed black on OD aircraft and in squadron colours and black on NMF. Group markings were yellow wing and tail bands, often outlined black, and each squadron applied badges to the cowling. Some aircraft had their numbers repeated on the wing leading edge, inboard of the guns and sometimes on the lower cowl lip.

The 'X' battle number prefix continued to identify P-47s of the 79th FG and some had red cowl rings. Late markings were medium blue tailplanes with three yellow lightning flashes on the vertical surfaces. Squadron badges were painted on the cowling in some cases.

Red cowl rings and occasionally, cowl flaps, and red/white horizontal tail stripes identified the 86th FG by mid-1944. Overpainted serials were often repeated in full or abbreviated form, under the cockpit on both razorback and later models. Squadron badges were also applied.

Both early and late model P-47s also carried colour markings in the 324th Group, squadrons being identified by a small pennant in the horizontal tail band — yellow, red and white for the 314th, 315th and 316th Squadrons respectively. These colours were also used for a small diamond on the cowling and a red lightning flash group marking appeared on the forward fuselage. Squadron badges were also applied in many cases.

The 325th 'Checkertails' also applied red to cowl rings, often outlined or swept-back on each side of the fuselage. The group's yellow and black checks adorned the entire tail-plane surfaces in most cases and battle numbers were usually white.

The 322nd FG used P-47s only for a short time and some only had the group's red tail decoration on OD finished machines.

The 350th FG identified its squadrons by diverse markings: the 345th had a black diagonal vertical tail band with yellow lightning flash, the 346th had black/NMF rudder checks and a large red A was employed by the 347th. Each squadron also had a number / letter / number fuselage

P-47D-30 44-20978 and a D-25 42-26540 in the 1945 markings of the 346th FS, 350th FG, 12th AF. The nearest machine is No 3 of 'C' Flight and the second, No 1 of 'B' Flight. It is possible that flight elements within the squadron were no longer necessary at war's end, hence the overpainting of 'Torrid Tessie's' 'C' to read as an 'O'.

code, the first being the last digit of the squadron number, the second the flight letter and the third the individual aircraft number.

A shortened form of the 350th Group's squadron coding was used by the 1st Grupo of the Brazilian Air Force, attached to the Group. Bubble canopy model P-47s were marked A1, B1, C1, etc, the first being the flight letter, the second the aircraft number. These characters were in white (black on NMF) and painted on the cowling. Each Brazilian aircraft had Medium Green and yellow rudder stripes and national insignia in standard USAAF locations.

20th Air Force The 413th, 414th and 507th Groups flew the P-47N under the direction of the 20th AF and were iden-

tified as follows — fin rudder diamond, heart and spade for the 413th's 1st, 21st and 34th Squadrons, with respectively A, B, and C squadron letters on the fuselage, followed by an aircraft number.

The 414th had yellow, black/yellow checks and light blue tail surfaces for its 413th, 437th and 456th Squadrons, with identification and cowl rings in the squadron colour.

Yellow tails identified aircraft of the 507th, with light blue for two squadrons — a open triangle for the 463rd, a diagonal stripe for the 464th and all-yellow for the 465th, often with a black border where the colour ended on the rear fuselage. The numbers 100-130, 131-169 and 170-199 identified individual aircraft in each squadron respectively.

Curtiss P-40 Warhawk

5th Air Force Dark Green and Earth camouflaged P-40Es as well as OD and NG finished machines were on the strength of the 49th Group for early operations from Australia. Diverted British contract machines carried black RAF serials and white fin numbers identified the squadrons — 1-39 for the 7th, 40-69 for the 8th and 70-99 for the 9th. A number of aircraft also sported striking personal emblems forward of the fuselage national

insignia, as well as sharkmouths.

By 1943, when Pacific theatre white tail and wing leading edge markings were applied, fin numbers were repositioned on the nose. Serials were usually left on OD patches. Squadron colours, blue for the 7th, yellow for the 8th and red for the 9th, were applied to spinners in a variety of patterns; the extreme lip of the nose intake was occasionally in white, or left in bare metal. Late in the war, P-40Ns of the 7th FS were to be seen with single

USAAF camouflage of World War 2

blue chordwise fin/rudder bands.

The 7th FS also included a flight of P-40s known as the 'Nip Nippers', with distinctive sharkmouths, complete with 'sabreteeth' and identified by fin numbers.

Machines of the 8th FG were identified by single letters, P-40K and N models of the 35th FS having them on the nose in yellow, the squadron colour. Where serials were not left on OD patches when white theatre markings were applied, they were repainted in black. Front spinner cones were in yellow and some machines had a coloured edging band to their sweptback tail markings where they terminated on the fuselage, probably red.

7th Air Force Serials and basic plane-in-squadron numbers identified early P-40Es of the 73rd FS of the 318th FG on Guadalcanal — markings common to most of the Pacific based fighter units until 1943. It was the 45th FS of the 15th FG that used an overall 'pink' on its P-40Ns, the actual shade probably being close to Sand. Serials were black and some aircraft carried the squadron emblem, a caricatured Red Indian riding a sharkmouthed fighter, on their lower nose

panels.

9th Air Force The first US P-40 unit in the MTO in 1942, the 57th FG flew both E and F models in at least three basic camouflage schemes — Sand upper-surfaces with Azure Blue undersides; Sand shadow shading over Olive Drab with Neutral Grey undersides and Middle Stone/Sand and Dark Earth with either blue or grey undersides. There were however, variations to these schemes, particularly when local paints were used.

Each of the 57th Group's squadrons (and those of the 79th and 324th Groups) had number blocks to identify its aircraft — 10-39 for the 64th FS, 40-69 for the 65th and 70-99 for the 66th. Each digit was split by the national insignia on both sides of the fuselage and respective 'Black Scorpions', 'Fighting Cocks' and 'Exterminators' badges were applied to the noses of many machines.

A similar numeral code was used by the 79th FG, with the addition of an 'X' prefix, forward of the number on the port side of the fuselage, aft on the starboard. The Group's 85th, 86th and 87th Squadrons were known respectively as the 'Flying Skulls', 'Com-

Typical American Volunteer Group markings on a P-40B with a red rear fuselage stripe identifying the 3rd Pursuit Squadron. British-type shadow shading of Dark Green and Dark Earth, with Sky undersides. The Chinese Nationalist insignia was carried on the wings only.

Curtiss P-40 Warhawk

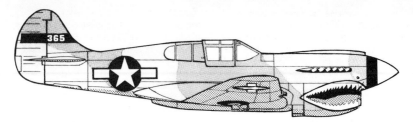

Curtiss P-40K of the 23rd FG, 14th AF. Dark Earth and Mid-Stone camouflage with Sky undersides. White three-digit serial on black tail band. Red, white and blue sharkmouth with black and white spinner.

A P-40F of the 66th FS, 57th FG, 12th AF. The RAF fin flash theatre marking obscures the first digits of the serial on the aircraft's Dark Earth and Stone camouflage (Howard Levy).

anches' and 'Skeeters', and badges were applied to most aircraft. Additionally, girl pin-ups were common on the rudders of P-40s of the 85th FS, where they often obliterated serial digits.

The 324th Group also applied numbers split by the national insignia, its prefix being a 'Y'. Squadron badges were not carried, a coloured horizontal diamond on the nose identifying each — yellow for the 314th, red for the 315th and blue for the 316th.

Most desert P-40s had the RAF fin flash theatre marking, as well as red spinners serving to emphasise their identity. The flash often covered the first/last digits of the serial, which was occasionally repainted on the rudder in yellow or black. The pin-ups of the 85th FS hid the remaining numbers and there seems to have been little need to present the serial elsewhere.

12th Air Force When the 9th AF reformed in the UK, the three P-40 units joined the 12th AF, which had the 33rd and 325th Fighter and 27th and 86th Fighter Bomber Groups assigned directly to it.

Few markings are believed to have been applied by the 33rd Group, the P-40Fs of which had the US flag painted on either side of the fuselage and below the port wing for Operation Torch. These markings were also carried by the 325th FG, which eventually adopted the numeral system used by the ex-9th AF groups, but grouped forward of the national insignia. Known as the 'Checkertails', the 325th also applied yellow and black checks to the fin/rudder and later the entire tail units of its aircraft. Initially, spinners were in squadron colours — yellow for the 317th FS, white for the 318th and red for the 319th, although

USAAF camouflage of World War 2

red spinners became general within a short time. It was a practice of the Group to add a small 'A' forward of the fuselage number, if two aircraft carried the same number.

Later markings of the 33rd FG appear to have been inconsistent, although the 58th, 59th and 60th Squadrons had respectively red spinners/tail bands, white tail stripes and yellow tail stripes specified, but not necessarily applied. Two-tone camouflage finish was applied to a number of 33rd Group aircraft during early months of combat.

Few details are known about the markings of the P-40 fighter bomber groups, apart from all-red tail units used by the 532nd FS of the 27th FBG.

Also seeing action in the MTO was the all-negro 99th FS which operated with the 33rd and 79th Groups before

The 'Black Scorpion' insignia of the 64th FS, 57th FG painted behind the red spinner, nose band and blaze of a P-40F.

being brought up to group strength in 1944 as the 322nd FG. P-40s of the 99th carried numbers split by the national insignia, with an 'A' prefix.

When bars were added to the US national insignia in mid-1943, the 99th often repainted its ID numbers over them. Other P-40 units, which had their numbers placed close to the old star marking, preferred to apply the new insignia to the wings only, at least until the paint shops could add the 'stars and bars' and group the number together forward of them.

11th Air Force Upon formation of the 11th AF in January 1942 — having been the Alaskan AF for about one month — P-40Es of the 11th FS were on hand for combat, to be followed by the 18th FS and 344th Squadrons, which in turn became part of the 343rd FG. Some P-40s were flown by the 54th FS, but P-38s were its main equipment. The 11th FS sported the well-known 'Bengal Tiger' nose markings on the majority of its machines, along with yellow spinners. Both Olive Drab and Earth and green camouflage was carried by aircraft of the 343rd Group and it is believed that each squadron adopted white rudder markings to identify each squadron — an 'L' shape for the 11th, a single vertical stripe for the 18th and a vertical with a short horizontal to form a cross for the 344th. Aircraft of the 11th also carried a second white stripe immediately behind the cockpit.

Two and three digit fin numbers, in

The early markings of the 80th FG seen on Warhawks in Burma. The aircraft have low tail numbers which probably indicated the 88th Squadron. Spinners were probably yellow, the skull marking being white.

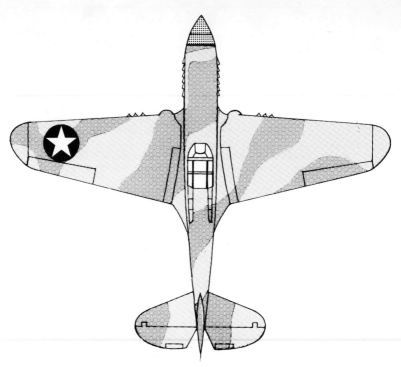

Plan view of camouflage pattern applied to USAAF P-40s in a number of theatres.

white and yellow, probably based on the serial, served as aircraft identification, and yellow spinners were common.

10th and 14th Air Forces The P-40B and C models of the American Volunteer Group were divided between the 1st, 2nd and 3rd Pursuit Squadrons, which carried white, blue and red fuselage bands respectively. Overall colour was mainly British type shadow shading of Dark Green and Earth, with Sky undersides. One or two-digit white plane-in-squadron numbers, probably 1-39 for the 1st PS, 40-69 for the 2nd and 70-99 for the 3rd, were painted on the fuselage.

The respective squadron emblems, the 'First Pursuit', 'Panda Bears' and 'Hell's Angels' were applied to nose or centre fuselage in various styles and some aircraft carried the full AVG 'Flying Tiger' badge.

Similar markings were carried by machines of the 23rd Fighter Group,

which replaced the AVG in mid-1942. Originally part of Chennault's China Air Task Force of the 10th AF, the 23rd flew aircraft with US national insignia painted out and Chinese Nationalist applied, although US insignia seems to have been re-applied after a short time, but on wings only. Three-digit numbers in the 100 range appear to have been used as plane-in-*group* identification, although rear fuselage identity bands, similar to those of the AVG, were used. The 23rd used most P-40 models before changing to P-51s, and some K models in the group had three-digit fin numbers applied on a black band where the original serial had been overpainted. Spinners were often halved in white and a squadron colour.

Similar camouflage and markings were employed by the 51st FG, although various OD and green upper surfaces were seen as the war progressed. The 51st used numbers and

USAAF camouflage of World War 2

P-40Fs of the 57th FG in Sand and Azure Blue finish. No 47 has the red spinner and diamond nose design sported by a number of machines of the group. The nose number was also red, along with the name 'Sally'. 'US ARMY' lettering appears under the wings in black and the fuselage numbers are outlined with black on each side of the insignia.

probably spinner colours to identify squadrons; numerals were placed on the fuselage side, forward of the national insignia. After transfer to the 14th AF, it is thought that the 51st adopted rudder letters as squadron identification, one of which used a letter C pierced by a small arrow, sabretooth sharkmouths and three-digit fin numbers.

The last CBI P-40 unit was the 80th FG, the aircraft of which carried unmistakable white skull designs on their noses in 1944. Prior to the application of the skull marking, the group used nose and fin/rudder numbers usually painted in yellow, possibly 1-25 for the 28th FS, 26-49 for the 89th, 50-75 for the 90th and 76-99 for the 459th Squadrons. The skull emblem was the badge of the 89th FS, but photographs indicate that all squadrons used it, as machines with numbers as low as 12 and as high as 73 carried it, and the whole group probably changed to a plane-in-group ID number system. The numbers were white in the majority of cases, positioned over the serial, although there were examples with the numbers applied over the serial. Spinners were

in a variety of shades.

13th Air Force Aircraft of the 18th Fighter Group on Guadalcanal in 1943 had standard OD and NG camouflage and it was not until a move was made to the Solomons that distinctive white recognition bands were used. In company with the 68th FS and RNZAF Warhawks, the 18th applied white tail theatre markings to P-40E, F, K and L models. A white vertical band was painted around the centre fuselage and a second immediately forward of the windshield to end at the wing root. Diagonal bands were painted from the gear leg housing on the wing leading edge to the tips on all four surfaces, bisecting the national insignia in a wide V shape. White numbers in the 100 range appeared on the lower nose. Front spinner cones were also white on many machines, the rear section often being left in OD.

With bars added to the national insignia, the 18th's P-40s did not initially have the blue surrounds, the bars often being thinner than stipulated, to match the width of the recognition bands. Incidentally, any kills scored in the 18th FG were credited to the aircraft, rather than the pilot.

Consolidated OA-10 Catalina

Although not engaged in a combat role with the USAAF, a total of 359 Catalinas were allocated Army serials during the war and, among other duties, they carried out the vital task of rescuing downed aircrews in both the Pacific and European theatres.

In the Pacific, the 5th AF had the 3rd and 6th Emergency Rescue Squadrons assigned, the 13th AF had the 2nd and the 4th ERS was based on Iwo Jima to support 20th Air Force operations. The 8th Air Force had the 5th ERS assigned.

Although the Catalina was not the only patrol and search aircraft type used by these squadrons, sea rescues could only be accomplished by the amphibians, one of which is depicted in the accompanying drawing. Apart from the dark blue and white scheme illustrated, Army Cats, or 'Dumboes' as they were called, were also overall white and probably black and Olive Drab and grey. Serials were either in standard yellow or black, depending on background colour; aircraft of the 2nd ERS carried the last two digits of the serial on the nose on a white panel as shown. Few other identity markings are known to have been used.

Consolidated OA-10A 44-33883 of the 2nd Emergency Rescue Squadron, 13th Air Force. Overall dark blue top surfaces with white below. Black aircraft number on white nose panel. Yellow serial and black/yellow tail tip stripes.

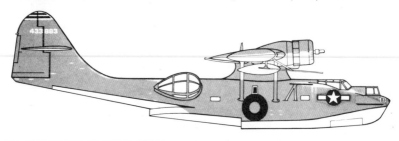

USAAF camouflage of World War 2

8th Air Force code letters

8th AF bomber squadron code letters

Group	Sqdn	Code	Aircraft
34	4	Q6	B-24
	7	R2	B-17
	18	8I	
	391	3L	
44	66	WQ	B-24
	67	NB	
	68	GJ	
	506	QK	
91	322	LG	B-17
	323	OR	
	324	DF	
	401	LL	
92	325	NV	B-17
	326	JW	
	327	UX	
	407	PY	
93	328	GO	B-24
	329	RE	
	330	AG	
	409	YM	
94	331	QE	B-17
	332	XM	
	333	TS	
	410	GL	
95	334	BG	B-17
	335	OE	
	336	ET	
	412	QW	
96	337	QJ	B-17
	338	BX	
	339	AW	
	413	MZ	
100	349	XR	B-17
	350	LN	
	351	EP	
	418	LD	
303	358	VK	B-17
	359	BN	
	360	PU	
	427	GN	
305	364	WF	B-17
	365	XK	
	366	KY	
	422	JJ	
306	367	GY	B-17
	368	BO	
	369	WW	
	423	RD	
351	508	YB	B-17
	509	RQ	
	510	TU	
	511	DS	
379	524	WA	B-17
	525	FR	
	526	LF	
	527	FO	
381	532	VE	B-17
	533	VP	
	534	GD	
	535	MS	
384	544	SU	B-17
	545	JD	
	546	BK	
	547	SO	
385	548	GX*	
	549	XA*	
	550	SG*	
	551	HR*	
389	564	YO	B-24
	565	EE	
	566	RR	
	567	HP	
390	568	BI	B-17
	569	CC	
	570	DI	
	571	FC	
392	576	CI	B-24
	577	DC	
	578	EC	
	579	GC	
398	600	N8	B-17
	601	30	
	602	K8	
	603	N7	
401	612	SC	B-17
	613	IN	
	614	IW	
	615	IY	
445	700	RN	B-24
	701	MK	
	702	WV	
	703	IS	
446	704	FL	B-24
	705	HN	
	706	RT	

Group	Sqdn	Code	Aircraft
	707	JU	
447	708	CQ	B-17
	709	IE	
	710	IJ	
	711	IR	
448	712	CT	B-24
	713	IG	
	714	EI	
	715	IO	
452	728	9Z	B-17
	729	M3	
	730	6K	
	731	7D	
453	732	E3	B-24
	733	E8	
	734	F8	
	735	H6	
457	748	RUW*	B-17
	749	JOB*	
	750	PPL*	
	751	MJA*	
458	752	7V	B-24
	753	J4	
	754	Z5	
	755	J3	
466	784	T9	B-24
	785	2U	
	786	U8	
	787	6L	
467	788	X7	B-24
	789	6A	
	790	Q2	
	791	4Z	
482	812	MI	B-17
	813	PC	B-24
	814	SI	
486	832	3R	B-24
	833	4N	
	834	2S	
	835	H8	
487	836	2G	B-24
	837	4F	
	838	2C	
	839	R5	
489	844	4R	B-24
	845	S4	
	846	8R	
	847	T4	
490	848	7W	B-24
	849	W8	
	850	7Q	
	851	S3	
491	852	3Q	B-24
	853	T8	
	854	6X	

Group	Sqdn	Code	Aircraft
	855	V2	
492	856	5Z	B-24
	857	9H	
	858	9A	
	859	X4	
493	860	NG	B-24
	861	Q4	
	862	8M	
	863	G6	

8th AF fighter squadron code letters

Group	Sqdn	Code	Aircraft
4	334	QP	Spitfire/
	335	WD	P-47/
	336	VF	P-51
20	55	KI	P-38/
	77	LC	P-51
	79	MC	
55	38	CG	P-38/
	338	CL	P-51
	343	CY	
56	61	HV	P-47
	62	LM	
	63	UN	
78	82	MX	P-47/
	83	HL	P-51
	84	WZ	
339	503	D7	P-51
	504	5Q	
	505	6N	
352	328	PE	P-47/
	486	PZ	P-51
	487	HO	
353	350	LH	P-47/
	351	YJ	P-51
	352	SX	
355	354	WR	P-47/
	357	OS	P-51
	358	YF	
356	359	OC	P-47/
	360	PI	P-51
	361	QI	
357	362	G4	P-51
	363	B6	
	364	C5	
359	368	CV	P-47/
	369	IV	P-51
	370	CR/CS	
361	374	B7	P-47/
	375	E2	P-51
	376	E9	
364	383	N2	P-38/
	384	5Y	P-51
	385	5E	
479	434	L2	P-38/
	435	J2	P-51
	436	9B	

USAAF camouflage of World War 2